WEIRD FACTS ABOUT CURLING

Strange, Wacky, Informative & Hilarious

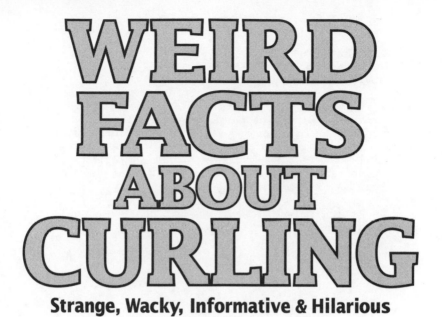

WEIRD FACTS ABOUT CURLING

Strange, Wacky, Informative & Hilarious

Geoffrey Lansdell

with contributions from
Carla MacKay

OVER
TIME
BOOKS

First printed in 2008 10 9 8 7 6 5 4 3 2 1
Printed in Canada

The Publisher: OverTime Books is an imprint of Éditions de la Montagne Verte

Website: www.overtimebooks.com

Library and Archives Canada Cataloguing in Publication

Lansdell, Geoffrey, 1977–
 Weird facts about curling : strange, wacky, informative & hilarious stories / Geoffrey Lansdell, Carla MacKay.

Includes bibliographical references.

ISBN-13: 978-1-897277-30-0
ISBN-10: 1-897277-30-X

 1. Curling—Miscellanea. I. MacKay, Carla, 1982– II. Title.

GV845.L35 2008   796.964   C2008-905383-4

Project Director: J. Alexander Poulton
Project Editor: Kathy van Denderen
Production: Alexander Luthor
Cover Image: Courtesy of Dreamstime; © Fallsview I Dreamstime.com

Photos Credits: Every effort has been made to accurately credit the sources of photographs. Any errors or omissions should be directed to the publisher for changes in future editions. Photographs courtesy of Photos.com (p. 20, p. 23, p. 47, p. 51, p. 57, p. 95, p. 105, p. 151, p. 181); Dreamstime.com (p. 53, p. 60).

We acknowledge the financial support of the Government of Canada through the Book Publishing Industry Development Program for our publishing activities.

PC: P5

Canadian Patrimoine
Heritage canadien

Contents

Curler's Code of Ethics 7

Introduction 8

Chapter 1: Curling Fundamentals 11

Chapter 2: Little-Known Stories from the World of Curling 25

Chapter 3: Elements of the Sport. 46

Chapter 4: The Strangest Quotes from the World of Curling 64

Chapter 5: Sticks and Stones 75

Chapter 6: Classic Curling Characters 103

Chapter 7: The Greatest Moments in Curling History 140

Chapter 8: Curling Lingo. 151

Chapter 9: Curling Time Line. 170

Appendix I: The Stats 204

Notes on Sources 252

Dedication

I would like to dedicate this book to Irene Hoffman, my beautiful grandmother. At 98 years old, she lives in Sidney, BC, where she spends her time watching the Brier, the Tournament of Hearts and Saskatchewan Roughrider football. In her younger days, she lived in the little Saskatchewan towns of Lake Lenore, Kerrobert, Humboldt and Yorkton. She is the toughest person I know, a wonderful storyteller, and she has inspired my mind, helping me imagine what drives the curling hotbed of the Canadian prairies.

–Geoffrey Lansdell

Curler's Code of Ethics*

I will play the game with a spirit of good sportsmanship.

I will conduct myself in an honourable manner both on and off the ice.

I will never knowingly break a rule, but if I do, I will divulge the breach.

I will take no action that could be interpreted as an attempt to intimidate or demean my opponents, teammates or officials.

I will interpret the rules in an impartial manner, always keeping in mind that the purpose of the rules is to ensure that the game is played in an orderly and fair manner.

I will humbly accept any penalty that the governing body at any level of curling deems appropriate, if I am found in violation of the Code of Ethics or rules of the game.

*Canadian Curling Association

Introduction

Curling is a Canadian game. Sure, it has Scottish roots, but just because a few Scotsmen hurled stones across a frozen loch in the early 16th century doesn't make it their game. Like many sports, curling has bloomed on foreign soil. Just think of basketball. At the end of the 19th century, a Canadian doctor by the name of James Naismith invented basketball by cutting holes in peach baskets; but we don't claim to own the sport. Basketball has come of age in the United States, while curling has evolved in Canada.

In this book, we explore the sport of curling by telling tall tales about the roaring game. We wander through its history, pausing every once in a while to shed some light on a few curling legends who have contributed to curling lore. We unveil the game's classic characters by telling their stories; we see how our heroes and heroines have brought the hammer down at crunch time; and we glimpse behind the scenes in an effort to understand the game's inner psyche.

Curling, however, is a social as well as a competitive sport. In an increasingly secular era, the curling rink is often where town and country come together. Still today, there are many communities across Canada that meet at the curling rink to chew the fat, to share local gossip, to talk politics or religion or sports. As a slow and strategic game, curling promotes conversation—conversation between players, between teams, between fans and between announcers.

The curling community also boasts some of the most ethically savvy minds you will find on Canadian soil. Curlers, whether amateur or professional, are characteristically patient, analytical, critical and fair. They can also be laconic and ironic. But once they hit the curling club for a post-game drink, all bets are off. The curling club is where the shenanigans begin and the game never ends. Like a pub and a hockey locker room rolled into one, the curling club is where you go to relish your glory or to drown your sorrows.

In the modern incarnation of curling, however, where advertising dollars, televised prestige and technology have joined forces to render the sport more exciting, more competitive and more rule-governed, there is a growing gap between the club level and the professional level. As a result, not only is the quality of play higher than it has ever been, but the sport is now spreading into non-traditional curling markets.

As a result of the inevitable onset of such changes, curling now finds itself at a fascinating crossroads. As one generation of fans (the baby boomers) slowly gives way to another more impatient generation, the curling rank and file is facing some stiff marketing challenges. In a nutshell, the marketing problem revolves around a central paradox: how do you cater to younger, more ethnically diverse fans without neglecting the older Anglo-Saxon demographic who are your bread and butter?

The problem has no clear solution, but it is evident that curling is on the rise. In researching this book, we have discovered that curling already has a marvelous legacy that is full of unique characters, odd stories of conquest and tragic tales of failure and defeat. Since 1998, it has been a full-medal Olympic sport, and there is no doubt that its profile will soar during the 2010 Olympics in Vancouver when the world's eyes are on Canada and its curlers. And now that the Brier and the World Curling Tour seem to have ironed out their differences, the future is as bright as sunlight on ice.

Chapter One

Curling Fundamentals

The Real Origins of the Game

Like many sports, pegging down an official date as to when the first game of curling took place is rather difficult. It's not as if one day a Scotsman woke up and said, "Hey, I got a bonny idea. Let's go outside on the frozen loch and throw a bunch of rocks into a circle." A more plausible idea is that curling evolved from a collection of other pastimes into the game we all know and love to this day. The unfortunate truth is that the history of curling is rather clouded and rough, like the ice surface the sport is played on, making the true origins and creators of the game somewhat difficult to identify.

What we do know is that a similar game was developed, called Eisschiessen (ice-shooting), sometime during the Middle Ages in the German-speaking areas of Europe. The game involved players sliding stones along a sheet of ice towards a target at the other end. Although it may sound like curling, Eisschiessen used a different system for scoring, and the players could choose from a variety of stones in different shapes and sizes. The game remained a purely folk pastime until the 20th century when the first championships were organized in Austria. (See Chapter Two to read about a famous Eisschiessen player.) The sport received international exposure in 1936 when it was added as a demonstration sport for the Winter Olympics in Germany.

Another sport similar to curling was played for centuries on the other side of the world on the ice of the cold Mongolian plateau. Called Moson Shagai Kharvakh, the game consisted of players tossing stones or small ice blocks at targets placed on a sheet of ice. Although there are similar sports around the world that share their roots with curling, the modern game differs greatly from all of the above. So where *did* curling get its first start?

Many historians note that Dutch painters Pieter Bruegel and Jacob Grimmer depicted a game that resembled curling in a series of paintings done between 1565 and 1575, but the game they were likely portraying was Eisschiessen. All elegant theories of curling's complicated lineage can be put aside, because without a doubt, it is the Scottish who are the tried and true inventors of the game—end of discussion!

The Scottish were first introduced to the game by Flemish craftsmen who travelled to the region during the 16th century, bringing with them a game akin to curling. Some of the earliest stones date to 1511. The Flemish might have brought the game to Scotland, but it was the Scots who embraced curling and turned it into the international sensation it is today. As the game took hold among the Scottish population, the first curling clubs began to spring up. The most famous and influential club that performed a significant role in the development of the game was the Duddingston Curling Society, established in 1795. The club was instrumental in clarifying the rules of the game and spreading curling to other parts of Scotland and beyond.

Factspiel

The Scottish originally dubbed curling the "roaring game" because of the sound the rock made as it slid down the pebbled ice surface.

By the 18th century, curling had become such a large part of Scottish folklore that it even infiltrated the songs the people sang and the tales they spun. It is a common anthropological observation that something of major importance to a culture is usually well celebrated and given much reverence. With well over 400 songs and ballads dedicated to the game of curling and to those who braved the cold temperatures of the frozen windswept lochs and moors, it is easy to make the connection that curling was deeply ingrained into the Scottish consciousness early on. Below are several examples of just how passionate the people were for their favourite game on ice. (If you have trouble understanding the language, try reading the passages out loud. It will help the Scottish-ly challenged.)

"Curling Song" by Dr. Henry Duncan

The music o' the year is hush'd,
In bonny glen and shaw, man;
And winter spreads o'er nature dead
A winding sheet o' snaw, man.
O'er burn and loch, the warlike frost,
A crystal brig has laid, man;
The wild geese screaming wi' surprise,
The ice-bound wave ha'e fled, man.
Up, curler, frae your bed sae warm,
And leave your coaxing wife, man;
Gae get your besom, tramps and stane,
And join the friendly strife, man.
For on the water's face are met,
Wi' mony a merry joke, man;

The tenant and his jolly laird,
The pastor and his flock, man.
The rink is swept, the tees are mark'd,
The bonspiel is begun, man;
The ice is true, the stanes are keen,
Huzza for glorious fun, man!
The skips are standing at the tee,
To guide the eager game, man;
Hush, not a word, but mark the broom,
And tak' a steady aim, man.
There draw a shot, there lay a guard,
And here beside him lie, man;
Now let him feel a gamester's hand,
Now in his bosom die, man;

Then fill the port, and block the ice,
We sit upon the tee, man;
Now tak' this in-ring, sharp and neat,
And mak' their winner flee, man.
How stands the game? Its eight and eight,
Now for the winning shot, man;
Draw slow and sure, and tak' your aim,
I'll sweep you to the spot, man.
The stane is thrown, it glides along,
The besoms ply it in, man;
Wi' twisting back the player stands,
And eager breathless grin, man.
A moment's silence, still as death,
Pervades the anxious thrang, man;
When sudden bursts the victor's shout,

With holla's loud and lang, man.
Triumphant besom's wave in air,
And friendly banters fly, man;
Whilst, cold and hungry, to the inn,
Wi' eager steps they hie, man.
Now fill ae bumper, fill but ane,
And drink wi' social glee, man,
May curlers on life's slippery rink,
Frae cruel rubs be free, man;
Or should a treacherous bias lead
Their erring course ajee, man,
Some friendly in-ring may they meet,
To guide them to the tee, man.

In the above work, we clearly see thoughtful and heartfelt passion for curling and love for the game's atmosphere. As soon as old man winter's breath freezes the waters of the loch, a voice calls out, for it is the time to curl. Friends gather and talk of innocent things, but when it comes time to toss the first rock, silence automatically falls, and all attention turns to the game. The author of the poem was clearly a lover of the game.

Famed poet and bard of the Scottish people, Robert Burns never attempted a game of curling that we know of, but he did reference the game when he wrote a poem for his friend Tam Samson after Tam passed away.

"Tam Samson's Elegy" by Robert Burns

When winter muffles up his cloak,
And binds the mire like a rock;
When to the loughs the curlers flock,
Wi' gleesome speed,
Wha' will they station at the cock?
Tam Samson's dead!

He was the king of a' the core,
To guard, or draw, or wick a bore,
Or up the rink like Jehu roar
In time o'need;
But now he lags on death's hog-score:
Tam Samson's dead.

True curlers can never leave the game on the ice; it gets into their blood and inhabits their dreams, and for the religious curler, there is even a prayer to be said before meals.

Curler's Grace 1

O'Lord wha's love surrounds us a'
And brings us a' the gether
Wha writes your laws upon oor hearts
And bids us help each ither

We bless Thee for Thy bounties great
For meat and hame and gear
We thank Thee, Lord, for snaw and ice
But still we as for mair

Gi'e us a heart to dae whit's richt
Like curlers true and keen
To be guid friends along life's road
And soop oor slide aye clean

O'Power abune whose bounty free
Oor needs and wants suffices
We render thanks for Braley Bree
And meat that appetises

Be Thou our Skip throughout life's game
An' syne we're sure to win
Tho' slow the shot and wide the aim
We'll soop each ither in.

(From the Royal Caledonain Curling Club)

Curler's Grace 2

O Power abune whose bounty free
Our needs and wants suffices.
We render thanks for barley bree
And meat that appetises.

Be thou our skip throughout life's game
An' syne we're sure to win,
Tho' slow the shot and wide the aim
We'll soop each ither in.

Songs and yarns aside, it is clear that the Scottish were the ones to embrace and nurture curling, while establishing its rules and turning the game into an obsession that they then spread around the world. And the first place outside the British Isles to fervently embrace curling was the New World. As author Doug Maxwell so elegantly observed in his book *Tales of a Curling Hack*, wherever Scots settled, they introduced curling to their newly adopted country. "Today, you could open up the phone book and pick out all the McHaggises and MacDiddlys,...and you would be reasonably certain there would be Scottish curlers somewhere in the listing."

Curling in North America

Throughout the 18th and 19th centuries, as curling became ingrained in the consciousness of the Scots, expatriates of the British Empire began to establish a place for curling within the New World. The Scots, of course, could not do without their favourite pastime, and as luck would have it, the northern and therefore colder regions of the New World provided the perfect conditions to continue their traditions.

The first evidence of curling in North America lands squarely in Canada. The accepted story is that the game first appeared in the east when the Scottish 78th Fraser Highlanders of the British Royal Army joined General Wolfe in fighting the French in Québec City in 1759. The common lore is that during the lengthy battle on the Plains of Abraham, in the winter months when soldiers

Curling has always been big in Banff. Its curling club has been around since 1899, but in the early years, its members went to beautiful spots like the Banff National Park to play a game.

had little else to do, the Scottish soldiers took up a traditional game of curling on the frozen waters of the St. Charles River. Although no cannonball curling rock was left for historical record, it was written that the soldiers melted down cannonballs and reshaped them into curling rocks.

When the war ended and many of the soldiers put down roots in the country, curling began to take hold throughout much of what became known as the Dominion of Canada.

Factspiel

The oldest curling club in North America is the Royal Montréal Curling Club. The club was founded in 1807 and continues to function to this day.

The Scottish may have created and nurtured the game, but it was the Canadians who fully embraced curling and turned it into the professional sport it is today—with around one million curlers and an even bigger television audience during the Brier competition.

The Physics of Curling

It might seem like a simple game, but with curling there is always more than meets the eye. Down at your local curling club, players are too busy planning their next shots to think about what goes on when they launch their rocks down the ice. But when you take a close look at the physics of curling, a lot is happening that you might not have realized, so pay attention, because the following information just might help your game.

Every curler knows that when a rock is turning counter-clockwise, it curls to the left, but few know how and why this happens. However, not all rotating spheres perform the same way when thrown. There is something special about a 42-pound stone travelling down the ice that makes it do what it does. If you don't believe it, take a regular drinking glass, turn it on its side and slide it counter-clockwise over a smooth surface. Go ahead, try it. Well, notice anything? While a curling stone that is spun counter-clockwise will rotate to the left, the glass will turn to the right. What is going on here? You might think that both the glass and curling rock would rotate in the same direction, given that they are both spun in a counter-clockwise direction, but in curling, there are a few more physical forces at play that make the rock behave the way it does.

First, let us understand why the glass "curls" to the right whereas the curling stone curls to the left when both are turned counter-clockwise. When the glass is spun, it will tend to tip forward. This puts pressure on the front of the glass, leaving the back of the glass with less friction. Thus, while the glass moves counter-clockwise, the friction on the front of the glass is greater than the friction on the rear of the glass, thereby forcing the glass to the right. So why doesn't a curling stone do the same? Both the glass and the curling rock are given the same spin, with about the same amount of surface area contact, so they should follow the same physics, right? Well, the most important thing to remember is that curling is played on ice.

When the curling stone is released, it acts under the same forces as the glass when it is turned. The rock should naturally exert more pressure on the front of the rock as it spins down the ice, but in fact it is the back of the stone that

Before taking a shot, players clean the underside of the stone to clear away any debris it might have picked up that could steer the shot astray.

takes the most friction. This occurs because the initial pressure on the front of the rock continually melts the ice beneath it, momentarily increasing the weight on the back of the stone. Therefore, in the counter-clockwise motion, the sideways motion at the back is to the right, and the friction acting against it forces the stone to the left. But as the astute curler knows, the ordinary curling stone is capable of so much more.

Have you ever noticed that when a curling rock slows down it tends to curl a lot more than when it is moving faster? This occurs because there is a lot less friction on the front as the rock slows down, and much more friction on the back, so the momentum forces the rock to curl more. But what is physically happening to the rock and to the ice? The key to the answer is in the ice and on the rock's running edge (the part of the rock that touches the ice).

As the stone moves along the ice surface, it slightly melts the ice, forming a thin layer of water just beneath the running edge. Because of the rotation of the rock, the running edge tends to carry some of that water with it. This thin layer of water gets dragged along with the rock as it moves down the ice. As the rock begins to slow down, the water is dragged from the back and makes its way to the front—this is why there is less friction on the front than the back, therefore explaining why the rock tends to curl more as it slows down.

Chapter Two

Little-Known Stories from the Curling World

The Terminator's Curling Lineage

Quickly picture an image of Arnold Schwarzenegger's father. Got it? OK, good. Now, I assume that most of you pictured an incredibly large hulk of a man, whose hands and face show the lines of a hard but well-lived life. That description fits perfectly with the image we have of his son, who destroyed armies and civilizations in his films. But here's the reality: the Terminator's father was often dressed in a wool curling sweater, complete with club crest, holding his favourite broom stick. Not the tough image you might imagine, but Gustav Schwarzenegger was one of the top curlers in Austria. Actually, he played a game very similar to curling but under a different name in Austria, called Eisschiessen. During his best years in curling, Arnold's father was part of the team that won Austria's national championships. But instead of sweeping the ice and knocking out rocks like his father, Arnold chose to sweep away bad guys and knock off heads.

It's All About the Pins

If one thing is consistent about all curlers, it's that they are die-hard pin collectors. Each pin on a curler's jacket proudly displays a moment in that curler's life; like a Scout's badge, each one represents a specific accomplishment, and in curling they have a pin for everything.

Curlers can get a pin for just showing up at a bonspiel or winning a draw during the season, or they trade pins with friends. Handing out pins might seem like a strange way to reward someone, but as any passionate curler knows, they are part of the tradition of the game, as a way to remember a specific tournament and the people they met along the way. Each pin tells a story of an amazing win, an incredible shot or simply a good time.

Take a trip to almost any curling rink, and you will notice two events taking place: the curling on the ice, and the trading and collecting of pins. Prices can range from a few dollars to well into the hundreds for the more collectable ones.

If you doubt the importance or significance of the pin culture in curling, you simply have to pay a visit to the Turner Curling Museum in Weyburn, Saskatchewan, which proudly displays over 18,000 curling pins from across Canada and around the world.

Curling and the Church

Curling and religion might seem to be able to co-exist in harmony, but over the history of the game there have been a few documented run-ins between the two practitioners. It wasn't that the church objected to curling on any religious or spiritual grounds (although I am sure some of the more hard-line zealots would find a problem with the cashspiel). In fact, those of the cloth were some of the first curlers. How better to keep the body warm and in shape during a cold Scottish winter? The church objected to curling

Before curling reinvented itself as an equal opportunity sport, it was a good old Victorian game in which the men curled; the women watched; and both were dressed to the nines.

because it could only be played when most people had a day off, and that day was Sunday. For some it was, "And on the seventh day He rested"; for others it was, "And on the seventh day he curled."

Not all churches observed the strict attendance for Sunday services, but a few parishes in Scotland and Canada had to keep a close watch over their flocks, because a clean sheet of ice on a cold winter day was always a temptation for the curling lover. Often, it was curling that the flocks chose over church, raising a few disgruntled eyebrows in the clergy.

In Scotland, the most vilified (at the time) and famous case of church versus curling occurred in 1638, when someone was found curling on the Sabbath, and to add insult to injury, he just happened to be a member of the clergy.

What follows below is a fictionalized account of an actual story of the Bishop of Orkney and how his passion for curling got him into trouble. There existed only a short mention of this incident in a church ledger so the author has taken a few liberties with the story to liven it up, but I believe it to be an accurate representation.

The Short Story of Bishop Graham

One cold winter Sunday morning on the scenic Scottish Orkney Isles, the Bishop

Graham of Orkney awoke and got up to look out the window.

A chill ran through the bishop's body as he approached the window.

The temperature had dropped overnight and frosted over the pane of glass that looked out over one of the most beautiful views in all of Scotland. But this morning, all he could see through his heavy eyelids and the frost-covered window was a cold white blur where the dark watery loch normally would appear.

He pushed out a breath of warm air onto his hands and then wiped away the frost.

Peering through the blinding light reflected off the fresh layer of snow, he could see the shapes of men from the village moving about down on the ice. On a cold, sunny, Sunday morning, the bishop knew exactly what they were doing.

An inner battle between duty and self-interest, between faith and fun, began to stir within the bishop. He had duties to perform; he had people counting on him; how could he simply abandon them to satisfy his own desires. But yet how could he pass up the perfect curling conditions. The cold and ice were conspiring against him to forego his duties. He decided he would go down to the loch to see the conditions of the ice for himself.

After getting washed and dressed, the bishop made his way down to the loch.

Stepping out into the cold and the fresh air, he quietly whispered a prayer that the ice would not provide the perfect conditions for curling lest he should have to miss his duties as a man of the cloth. He spoke just loud enough to ease his conscience but faint enough so that he thought God might not hear.

On his way down to the water, the bishop passed several people who wished him a good morning and said that they looked forward to the Sunday services.

"Morn' Bishop. Lovely day for a curl!" said Joseph, one of the local merchants with whom the bishop often curled.

The bishop saw the wry smile on his face. Joseph knew that the bishop was going down to see if the ice was good for curling; he knew exactly just how much the bishop would rather be curling than anything else. But the bishop responded with a short answer, not wanting to give away any of the excitement that welled within.

"Morn' Joseph. Thank you."

When he finally reached the edge of the loch, he walked out onto the ice and instinctively knew that it was a perfect day for curling. The temperature had dropped fast enough and with little wind to freeze the ice so that it was perfectly hard and smooth with few air pockets or cracks to disturb the delivery of the rocks. In all his years of curling, Bishop Graham had never seen conditions this perfect.

He let out a sigh, looked to the sky and appealed to the higher power, asking why his faith must be tested so.

"I am a faithful man filled with love and devotion for you my Lord. But I am still a man, susceptible to temptation. Is it a sin to appreciate your beautiful creation on this, the most perfect of all days?" he thought to himself.

Bishop Graham paused for a second as if waiting for an answer before returning to his room to get his scarf and gloves and anything else he would need to curl for the next few hours.

Elsewhere in the parish, the flock began to gather inside the church for the start of Sunday services. It wasn't long before people began to notice that Bishop Graham was absent from the regular Sunday service. Well acquainted with his passion for curling, it wasn't hard for most to figure out where the bishop was hiding.

Unfortunately, Bishop Graham's brothers of the cloth did not take the commitment to their duties to the Lord and his flock as capriciously as he had in choosing to curl over attending church. Above all, he chose Sunday, the Sabbath, to forego his duties. This was a direct violation of the laws of the church, and there would have to be consequences for contravening the will of God.

Four or five hours later, when the cold had penetrated to his bones and his teeth began to shudder, Bishop Graham decided that it was time to come in from the cold. After all, he had won a few games against some of the other men of the village and did manage one impossible triple takeout that he would surely be talking about for years to come. Only after he returned home and sat down by the fire to enjoy the day's pursuits did he suddenly remember his sacrifice. The bishop knew that it would not be difficult to figure out why he had been absent from the Sunday service, but he had hoped that his fellow clergy members would tolerate this minor indiscretion; after all, it wasn't every day that the perfect conditions on the loch presented themselves for curling.

A few days later, after he had eaten his dinner, he received the answer to his question.

There was a knock at his door. It was Father Mitchell. For a brief moment he breathed a sigh of relief because he knew Father Mitchell to be quite the curler, so any news that he had could only be good-tempered in nature. After exchanging pleasantries, Father Mitchell's expression changed from one of welcome to one of dread.

"I, unfortunately, must be the emissary who brings you bad news my brother," said Father Mitchell. "Your absence at the Sunday services, I am afraid, did not go unnoticed. It has been decided that you must appear before an assembly to answer for your sins."

Father Mitchell handed Bishop Graham the parchment, got up and left the room without another word. Bishop Graham did not have to open the letter to know that he was being called before the Glasgow Assembly of Presbyterians to answer for his transgressions. It wasn't every day that an assembly in Glasgow was called, so Bishop Graham knew he had committed a serious offence in their eyes and that he would have to answer for his actions.

As he sat down and opened the letter he laughed to himself as he read the serious tone of the document. "So much trouble for such a simple game," he said out loud.

But Bishop Graham was first and foremost a man of the cloth, and he respected the rules and restrictions of a life given to the service of God.

The next morning after packing his bags for the trip to Glasgow, he put on his warm coat, grabbed his favourite hat and took one last look down at the frozen loch where several men from the village were just starting to prepare the ice for a game of curling. He closed his bedroom door behind him and went into the street where a carriage was waiting to take him to Glasgow.

Bishop Graham knew by the sheer amount of people gathered for the assembly that they had other matters to consider above his simple indiscretion of curling on the Sabbath, to which he was slightly comforted. But when a booming voice broke the silence calling the meeting to order, Bishop Graham's stomach tightened.

"Order, Order," called one of the priests. "Let us begin this assembly with the case of one Bishop Graham of Orkney. He is being called before this assembly to answer for a violation of the laws of the Sabbath and for providing a bad example to the people in the parish. Bishop Graham, please come and stand before God to tell us of your transgressions."

"Gentlemen, I want to first say that my devotion to God and my flock has never wavered in over 30 years as a man of the cloth. For years I have devoted my life and soul to God's service and have unquestioningly performed my duties without fault or flaw. I have been called here before you today to answer for disregarding the strict observance of the Sabbath. As a man of the cloth I should have known my duty to the church comes first, and for that

I am ready to receive whatever judgment this assembly sees fit." Bishop Graham paused to take a breath.

"I am a man and therefore I am weak. My passion for the game of curling overcame my duty to the church, and for that I am truly sorry. The day presented the perfect conditions for the game, and temptation simply got the better of me. Gentlemen, please punish my violation of my duties, but do not place judgment on what I did."

Bishop Graham finished delivering his plea and sat back down. He hoped his words would find patient ears. After all, there certainly must be one curler among the assembly members.

The assembly left the room and returned a short time later with their decision.

"Bishop Graham of Orkney, this assembly has heard your words and considered them," said one priest. "We recognize your long service to the church and to the observance of your duties; however, we are bound by rules of the church and by the laws of God. Foregoing your duties on the Sabbath is a sin and cannot be overlooked. Let it be written down so that others may know that Bishop

Graham of Orkney is accused of the sin of curling on ice on the Sabbath. You shall return to Orkney and in a month's time you will be stripped of your position. I'm sorry it had to be this way."

Exiting the assembly, Bishop Graham could only wonder what might come as his punishment. Just as he was about to step into a waiting coach, a priest from the assembly came running up to him.

"Bishop Graham, I heard your story and found it disheartening. While I believe that you did truly violate the Sabbath, I am conflicted because I too am a curler and have been torn by your same dilemma on several occasions. Where can that leave men like you and I?"

Bishop Graham jumped into the coach and turned to answer the young priest. "You could say that curling was as much for the pleasures of the spirit as it is for the pleasures of the flesh. The problem for us is that we must choose."

Just as in Scotland, early Canadian curlers often came into conflict with their local parishes. The church felt that curling had its place in

Canadian society but not when the game interfered with the strict observance of the Sabbath. So in the battle between faith and curling, the church found that it was losing more of their parishioners, who preferred to be out on the ice on a Sunday morning rather than in the pews.

Because saving souls is a serious business, the church used its broad influence in the country to effect change of its own. Since it could not make people follow the laws of God, then they might listen to the more immediate laws of society.

In 1888, the Lord's Day Alliance was created under the sponsorship of the Presbyterian Church of Canada in order to fight the increasing secularization of the Sabbath. In the early phases of industrialized Canada, Sunday was the only day of rest for most workers, and the church noticed that people were opting to spend their time in secular pursuits rather than in the service of God, and as technology improved, the competition for people's time only grew more difficult for the church. The advent of electricity brought brand-new products into the home, and the popularity of motor vehicles allowed people to travel greater distances, to visit distant relatives or to spend time at a beach on Sundays, which put less people in the pews. Many Canadians couldn't decide whether to spend their time in recreation or religion. Because one of the major recreational pursuits of Canadians during the winter happened to be curling, the game came into the crosshairs of the church.

In 1903, a visiting Scottish curling team found itself embroiled in the controversy when they made a stop in Toronto. Being from Scotland, the curlers were aware of the church's position on the Sabbath, but they didn't think they would have the same problem in Canada.

Arriving in Toronto on a Sunday, the Scottish curlers knew they would not curl that day, especially since their captain was one Reverend John Kerr. Instead, they took the opportunity to visit Niagara Falls. But when Reverend Dr. Milligan of Toronto got wind of the Scottish curlers' plans, he vehemently criticized them from his pulpit for not observing the Sabbath, even though they were just visiting a tourist site. Angered over the public chastising, Reverend Kerr responded with a scathing letter to the editor in *The Globe* newspaper on January 26, 1903.

Rev. Mr. Kerr to the Editor of *The Globe*

I see in your issue of today that Rev. Dr. Milligan of St. Andrew's Church, Jarvis Street, has been making some severe strictures from his pulpit on the visiting of

Niagara Falls by the Scottish team of curlers on Sunday. He says the members of the team ought to be ashamed of themselves, and if there was a minister among them the matter was still worse. In the absence of members of the team from the city I write on their behalf to say that I am sure no one had any idea that they would offend Dr. Milligan or anybody else by taking the opportunity that was offered them, of visiting one of the most wonderful and awe-inspiring works of the great Creator, whose majesty and glory are revealed in nature as well as in revelation, sometimes more attractively than in some of our churches, where "new presbyters is but old priest writ large."

Since we came to Canada our team has regularly attended church, and surely a day off to worship the Almighty at such a magnificent shrine might be permitted us without our being held up, with the minister at the head, for reprobation of the Toronto people by Dr. Milligan, whose censure becomes the only fly in the pot of ointment in the grand reception given us by our brother Scots and our Canadian cousins. I have no doubt that the doctor means well, but I venture as a minister to say that such narrow Judaistic conceptions as he seems to hold, in my opinion, do more harm to true religion than any visits of ours to Niagara on a Sunday can ever do. I pity the prospect of the churches in this great and promising country if they cannot go beyond the Rev. doctor's conception of good conduct and good taste. Since I render him the honour of "all the sages," the Rev. doctor will pardon me for slightly transposing a stanza from nature's great poet, Wordsworth, who was always a good Christian:

> One impulse from Niagara
> Will teach you more of man,
> Of moral evil and of good,
> Than Dr. Milligan.

> John Kerr,
> Captain of the Curling Team

It appeared that scolding people did not work, so the Lord's Day Alliance changed tactics and lobbied the federal government for help. The Alliance gained a valuable partner when they brought the French Canadian Catholic hierarchy on board and promised to lobby the government to legislate a weekly day of rest.

In 1906, with the weight of the French Canadian Catholic Church behind them, the Lord's

Day Alliance successfully lobbied the Liberal Party of Canada and their leader, Prime Minister Sir Wilfrid Laurier, to introduce the "Lord's Day Act" into Parliament. By limiting the operation of non-essential businesses and leisurely pursuits on the Sabbath, it was hoped that the Lord's Day Act would leave people with nothing to do but go to church.

The Act, which went into effect in March 1907, also set out to prohibit the playing of all sports, including curling. The only problem with the order was its enforcement. Keeping larger entities such as business and professional organizations closed on Sundays was one thing, but policing the curling rinks of the nation was an entirely different story. In the more religious parts of Canada, the Lord's Day Act was observed to some degree, but keeping a true curler away from the ice is not an easy task. Most of the religious curlers went to church in the morning and had their curling gear waiting for them in their vehicles.

But as time passed and the modern multicultural Canada that exists today began to emerge, the Lord's Day Act carried less and less weight. In 1985, with the establishment of the Canadian Charter of Rights and Freedoms, the Lord's Day Act was removed from the law, and curlers across the country rejoiced.

Wheelchair Curling

For the able-bodied person, it might seem impossible to conceive of a way that a person in a wheelchair could curl. After all, how could they slide down the ice on wheels? But it is exactly that sort of challenge that drove a few determined athletes to invent the relatively new sport of wheelchair curling.

Wheelchair curling got its start in Europe in the 1990s before making its way to North America in the new millennium. The sport received international recognition when it held its first worldwide competition in Switzerland in 2002 and was added as a medal sport to the 2006 Paralympic Games in Torino, Italy (Canada won the gold over Great Britain).

Although the purpose of the game is still to see who can get the most points by pushing their stones closest to the button, wheelchair curling obviously has a few minor differences. First, there is no sliding. The wheelchair curler remains firmly in place just short of the hog line and uses a long stick, similar to those used in shuffleboard, to deliver the stone to the house. Second, it is a little more difficult to finesse the picture-perfect shots, but the game is as exciting and filled with suspense as a regular game.

Nothing Says Curling Like a Bonspiel

In the wonderful world of curling, a lot of professional curlers seem to get their pants in a bunch if you call their sport a game. And then there are the bonspielers, who treat curling as a game that is rooted in fun. In essence, bonspielers are regular old stiffs like you and me who enter curling tournaments in order to share a few laughs and a few drinks, eat like there's no tomorrow and compete in the name of fun.

"But wait just a minute," you might be saying to yourself. "What in the name of all that's holy is a *bonspiel?* Here you are rambling on about *bonspielers*, and I don't even know what a plain-and-simple *bonspiel* is. Is that like the spiel proselytizing curlers give you when you first express an interest in their roaring game?"

As a matter of fact, the term "bonspiel" basically means "league game." It has Dutch roots: *spel* more or less means game, while *bond* means league or federation. But in Canada, "bonspiel" is a blanket term that covers any form of curling get-together. There are of course varying degrees of formality, but fundamentally, a bonspiel is an amateur curling tournament between clubs. Bonspiels usually don't cost much, and the prize for the winning team is occasionally so lame it seems like a booby prize. For instance, it is not uncommon to hear of bonspiel winners winning things such as blenders, bags of meat or steak knives.

But bonspielers don't tend to give a hoot about the prize. For them, playing in a bonspiel has more to do with the social elements. On the ice, there is competitive camaraderie. On one of the evenings, there is often a large banquet, possibly followed by a dance or some kind of spectacle to further lift the curlers' tipsy spirits. And then there's the phenomenon of "home hosting," which is when someone decides that the party's just getting started, so invites people home to kick it up a notch.

From the original term "bonspiel," there have also been several spin-offs to describe different styles of bonspieling. The most obvious is the "cashspiel," which is naturally more competitive, since money is on the line. Today, the most lucrative tournaments on the cashspiel circuit are included on the World Curling Tour. Although there are smaller cashspiels that many professional players don't enter, the Grand Slam cashspiels are now worth a hundred grand to the winning foursome.

Chapter Three

Elements of the Sport

Stones

Not all curling stones are created equal. In the game's first few years of existence, the rocks were nothing like the polished granite stones of today. They were oddly shaped and did not have the handle to give the stones rotation. The first recognizable curling stones were rather crude, blunt instruments. These early stones were mainly river rocks that had notches cut in them to give the curler something to grip. The notches carved at the base of the stone made it awkward to grip and near impossible to lift. Using stones of various sizes, shapes and weights meant that no shot could be taken with any certainty, and any good shots were made simply by luck. The heaviest curling stones in evidence weighed an incredible 100 pounds (45 kilograms), making the sport accessible for only the strongest. Players eventually realized that smooth round stones just slightly larger than a soccer ball were better than others. Rocks with these characteristics were then chosen, and players slowly shaped rocks into their desired form when the proper stone could not be found.

Although today every curling stone is made from granite, in the early years of the game, the stones were made from almost everything except granite. Rocks made from sandstone, shale, limestone and other materials were all tried, but none of them passed the curlers' test. Some rocks chipped easily; some rocks didn't curl; and some just plain didn't look good. It wasn't until the 20th century that curlers worldwide clued into the benefits of using granite stones. The tough consistency of the stone made it easier to shape, more resistant to chipping, easier to curl down the ice and, when polished, granite stones look very slick.

Although blue and red are the most common colours for stones at curling clubs, yellow and red are the standard colours in major tournaments.

Finding the right stone to suit your individual style of play is not easy. Most professionals break in their stones when they first get them because the running edge is too sharp and tends to bite the ice too much, which makes it difficult to judge each shot. Most stones have to be used several times before they are deemed ready for serious competition. But this is not to say that stones wear out easily. Some clubs still have and use stones that are close to 60 years old. (At a cost of $500 and up, they'd better last that long.)

Factspiel

The Stirling Stone, considered the Rosetta Stone of curling, is the oldest curling rock ever found. Saved from the bottom of a Scottish bog in Dunblane, Scotland, the rock is engraved with the date 1511, making it the earliest record of curling ever found. It is half the size of a modern curling rock, and grips are carved into the stone. The game played by that poor fellow whose rock broke through the ice in 1511 is a little different than what we see today, but the Stirling Stone provides physical evidence that a recognizable form of curling existed first in Scotland five centuries ago.

Because curling stones are expensive to replace, manufacturers came up with an ingenious method of ensuring that stones endure. The process is called pitting. The manufacturer drills a central core through the stone, like you would core an apple, and removes the core and then glues the core back into the stone. When the rim or running edge wears out completely, it can be replaced at less expense than having to replace the whole stone.

Brooms

The use of the corn broom in curling grew out of the need to clear snow off the ice, since curling in its infancy was played outdoors, where snow and frost regularly got in the way. As such, the original purpose of the broom was to clear debris out of the stone's path. But once the game moved indoors, curlers noticed that sweeping had a desirable secondary effect. By rapidly sweeping the broom against the ice, curlers eventually realized that the broom momentarily melts the ice in front of the stone, which in turn decreases friction between the ice and the stone. As a result of this decrease in friction, the stone's trajectory straightens, and the stone doesn't slow down as quickly. In terms of curling strategy, this means that if you don't deliver your stone with enough speed, or if it is spinning too quickly and will curl too much, sweeping feverishly will help mitigate these problems.

Naturally, there have been several advances in broom technology over the years. Shortly after the game moved indoors and the effects of friction were well known, the ordinary house broom was replaced by a narrower corn broom that had a leather insert in its centre to hold the broom's long corn fibres together. More dense and compact than a house broom, this curling broom allowed curlers to heat the ice a little more by heavily slapping the ice. The only problem with the slapping method was that it was a relatively slow and labour-intensive process when compared with what the push broom could do.

Brushes

Originally popular on the European curling scene, the brush (which is more commonly called a "push broom" or just "broom") did not make it over to North America until the late 1970s when Paul Gowsell initiated a new trend. As with helmetless hockey players, it took a while to phase corn brooms out of the game, even though the new push broom had several clear advantages over the old corn broom. First of all, the push broom was less likely to leave debris on the ice.

Although both models can lose bristles, leaving a long and relatively thick corn fibre on the ice is far more problematic than leaving a thin

Although still called a broom by most of the curling fraternity, the modern brush helps sweepers apply more pressure to the ice while also sweeping faster. Both of these factors briefly melt the pebbled ice, which decreases friction and helps the stone travel faster and straighter.

little fibre behind. Secondly, and more importantly, the push broom's shorter bristles—which can be made of hog hair, horse hair or synthetic fibre—allow sweepers to sweep faster and to push and lean into their brooms. Both of these features of the push broom help decrease friction between the ice and the stone at a much faster rate than you could with a corn broom. And finally, the push broom comes in very handy when sliding out of the hack, as most curlers now use their brooms as a balancing aid so they don't tip or wobble while delivering a shot.

Cram-pits

Long before the easy days of setting up in the hacks and launching yourself down the ice to deliver a shot, some crafty curler on the Scottish lochs invented the cram-pits. Basically, these were spikes or cleats that were attached to the bottom of shoes and worked much like the shoes of a baseball player or golfer. Cram-pits gave curlers a grip on the ice, which they needed to propel themselves down the ice to deliver a rock.

Cram-pits were a revolutionary invention in the world of curling, because before their existence, players on the frozen lochs of Scotland had to cut holes into the ice. This was not the safest means of propelling yourself down the ice, because the holes increased the chances that a player could fall through the ice when trying to deliver the heavy rock.

But there was one major flaw with the cram-pits. The metal spikes often chewed up the ice, which affected future shots. To solve the problem, cram-pits were taken off the soles of the players' shoes and melted into the ice to provide a hold for the players. It was this type of hack that was most commonly used in curling until 1985, when an inventive curler named Marco Ferraro created the rubber hack that has become the worldwide standard and competitive norm.

A view from the hack

The Ice

If you strap on a pair of skates and try to step onto the curling ice, you will notice two things: first, that you have raised the ire of the entire curling club, and second, that it is a bumpy ride.

Curling ice, like the game itself, is special. Before a big game, if a Zamboni came out and flooded the ice, it would provide the worst possible conditions for curling. Unlike hockey players, who need a softer, flatter surface of ice so that the blades of their skates can grip the ice, curlers need a much harder surface so that the ice doesn't chip away when hurling a 42-pound rock along it, and so that the ice doesn't melt too rapidly under the rock. To create a harder ice surface, a sheet of curling ice is kept three or four degrees colder than a standard indoor hockey rink. Curlers also need ice that is as close as possible to being perfectly level. Hockey ice is always imperfect—some areas are higher or lower than others, cracks tend to develop and get worse during the course of a game, and the ice collects bits of debris, such as pieces of stick or hockey tape.

The key difference between hockey ice and curling ice is the surface. If you have ever been to a curling club or watched a match on television, you might have noticed someone with a large water tank strapped to their back, onto which is attached a long hose with a showerhead of sorts at the end. This machine is one of the most important machines in curling, for it is in charge of pebbling. Although pebbling might not sound like much, it is what causes the rocks to roar and curl their way down the ice.

"Pebbling" refers to the tiny droplets of water that fall from the water tank and freeze on the ice below. The person responsible for pebbling, usually called the ice technician, walks up and down the rink, spraying the ice with hot water (although it might seem counterintuitive, hot water freezes faster than cold). It may look as if the technician is randomly spreading the "pebbles," but there is a method behind it all.

The pattern the technicians use is important. When they first started to pebble the ice, technicians simply tried to spread an even layer across the ice, but they soon realized that certain parts of the ice wore out faster than others. The experienced ice tech knows that the centre of the ice requires the most pebbles whereas the sides only need a sprinkling.

But why ruin a perfectly smooth sheet of ice with a bunch of tiny little speed bumps you might ask? You will find the answer on the bottom of the curling rock. There is a small concave cup on the bottom of the rock, and it is only the outer edge of this cup (about 3–7 millimetres wide) that comes into contact with the ice. If the ice was a perfectly flat surface, that little concave cup at the bottom of the curling rock would act like a suction cup, and the rock would die.

Factspiel

The pebbles are responsible for that distinctive sound that all stones make as they travel down the ice. The rough, bumpy surface creates friction between the stone and the ice, thereby making that familiar sound. If you listen carefully, it almost sounds as if the rock is saying "Currrlll!" At least that's what the Scottish thought, which is why they called their sport "curling." It just so happened that another central feature of the game is the curling motion of the stones.

Once you start playing the game, you might notice a strange figure lurking in the shadows watching each curler's every move. This person is more than likely the ice technician, keeping an eye out for people who are messing up his perfect ice. The ice technician's job is hard enough, taking care of things such as pebbling the ice, controlling the temperature and maintaining all the equipment used in a curling facility—that is why some get a little perturbed when they see curlers taking liberties with their playing surface.

Tips for Keeping the Ice Technician Happy

- Try to stay off the ice when not playing. Shoes tend to pick up dirt and other debris that could affect the trajectory of the stone.

- When delivering a shot, do your best to keep hands, knees, elbows or any other part of your body off the ice. This contact wears away at the pebbling and affects the shots for the remainder of the game.

- Make sure to clean your brush so that it doesn't work any debris into the ice when you sweep.

- And please, at all costs, avoid putting your Tim Hortons' coffee mug on the ice before

With three red stones in the house and no yellows in sight, the red team is lying three.

taking a shot. There is nothing worse for an ice technician than coffee stains.

If all these conditions are met, you will more than likely have a pleasant game of curling. But when the game is done and it is time to hit the lounge, the job of the ice technician starts all over again. While the curlers are in the lounge drinking, the technician is preparing the ice for the next game. His biggest challenge? Pebbling.

Play seven matches on one sheet of ice during the day, with the ice technician pebbling the ice before every match, and there will be a significant buildup of pebbles on the sheets. The question then becomes one of how to get rid of the mounds of pebbled ice. In hockey, when they want to resurface the ice, they bring out the Zamboni, which strips off a layer of ice and then puts down a thin coating of water. But in curling, only specific areas of the ice need to be stripped, so another ingenious invention was necessary to scrape the ice clean.

In the early days of curling, scraping the ice was done the old-fashioned way—by getting down on hands and knees and using a sharp hand tool and an experienced eye to level the ice. Luckily for the modern ice technician, someone invented an ice-scraping machine, nicknamed the Ice King. The Ice King shaves off the accumulated ice after each competition and levels off the playing field so that stones won't suddenly curl out-of-bounds.

Factspiel

Before the invention of the Ice King, ice technicians cleaned the ice using a simple method called burning. This process involved dragging a large metal beast of a machine with an attached heating coil across the ice. The idea was to melt the top layer of the ice so that dirt or debris floated to the top where it could be vacuumed up, leaving behind a smooth, clean sheet of ice. The problem was that the machine didn't pick up all the debris, it wasn't easy to handle and it left patches of uneven ice.

The Eye of the Hog

Once upon a time (prior to 1955), curlers enjoyed a certain freedom of movement when delivering a stone down the ice. With no rule that established a specific line for the release of a curler's rock, players could hold onto the stone as long as they wished, but even with no restrictions, few players made it to the first tee line. All sports, however, are constantly evolving, and when new technology or techniques arrive on the scene, changes need to be made, and curling is not exempt from that rule.

By the 1940s in Canada, curling had exploded in popularity. Players were constantly trying to find new ways to gain the advantage over their opponents. One big advantage for curlers is to be able to hold onto their stones for as long as they can, which helps them control the path of the stone rather than releasing it earlier. The new materials such as plastic and Teflon, when placed on the bottom of the player's slider, propelled them much farther down the ice than the traditional sliders. But since anyone could have the new sliders, some players began working on their delivery technique.

Players like Matt Baldwin, inventor of the Baldwin slide, and many others raised the ire of officials by sliding nearly the entire length of the ice.

Curling rocks resting on the quiet ice before the start of a
"roaring game"

To even out the playing field, the curling governing body established the hog line rule in 1955.
The rule made it impossible for extreme sliders to
play to the crowds. When the rule was first established, players had to come to a complete stop
before reaching the hog line, but because of the
new shoes and better sliding techniques, players
often sailed right through. The rule was amended
years later to allow players to slide over the hog
line, but they had to release the stone before it
reached the hog line.

To police this new rule, hog line judges were brought in to watch every delivery for any infraction. But when you give a human being the dull job of staring at a line, sometimes for hours on end, there are bound to be missed calls and plenty of mistakes. At first there were no objections to having a person judge whether a player crossed the line in the minor tournaments and bonspiels around the world, but when it came to major tournaments, national and international championships, and large-sum cashspiels, the stakes became too high for any errors.

It might sound like an easy task for the official—to simply watch the hog line to see whether the player has released the stone before crossing the line—but determining the exact moment the handle is clearly released is extremely difficult and has led to many harsh words ("Are you blind!" being the most popular.) One of the most blatant hog line controversies occurred during the 2001 World Championships in Switzerland in a semi-final game between Canada's Randy Ferbey and Switzerland's Andreas Schwaller.

When Ferbey was called for breaking the hog line once, no one at the championship thought twice about the infraction called by the Swiss line judge, but when Ferbey was judged to have crossed the line three times, some suspicions arose as to the loyalties of the judges. A side note to this story is that during other games in that same tournament, all the hog line calls were made against Swiss opponents.

To keep curlers from strangling the judges, a more objective system of detection needed to be created, so a search began in 2002 for a reliable method of detecting the hog line infractions. There were some early successes, but it wasn't until Garry Paulson, president of Startco Engineering Ltd. in Saskatchewan, who just happened to be a curler, noticed that one of his creations used in the potash mines of the province would be a perfect solution to the hog line problem. The invention was a digital, solid-state starter that aided in the transportation of ore via a conveyor belt.

Using sensors had been thought of earlier, but figuring out *when* the player actually released the rock's handle hadn't been resolved. Paulson had a solution. By placing a long magnetic strip under the ice along the hog line and imbedding a sensor in the stone's handle, the system knows exactly when a player releases the stone. A red light on the handle signals an infraction, and a green light signals a legal move, thereby leaving no room for arguments.

Paulson's invention was called "The Eye of the Hog," and it is now standard at all major national and international curling events.

Factspiel

Do you know what it means to "hog the rock?" No, it's not keeping the rock all to yourself. When it's said that a player has "hogged the rock," it means that the player's delivered rock failed to cross the hog line, and it is removed from play. If you "hog the rock" out on the ice, you will not only lose the stone, but you will also hear about it from your friends.

Chapter Four

The Strangest Quotations from the World of Curling

Not long ago, a cultural anthropologist of questionable credentials told the story of curling's origins, a game he rightly called "a refrigerated form of lawn bowling." According to his research, it all started rather accidentally in the stone home of a young Highland couple. The bride, eager to please her new husband, was baking her first haggis when all of a sudden the mound of meat rolled out of the oven, onto the floor and into the cellar. The groom, "being a man of frugal habits…salvaged the haggis, put a handle on it, and thus became the father of the first curling rock." His wife, we must sadly note, left him the next day.

From these humble 16th-century origins, curling has of course made quite an impression on Canadian men and women. But in the beginning, the curling bug was a uniquely male affliction. By the middle of the 20th century, sociologists across the land had documented the inexplicable phenomenon of men's fascination with brooms. In these early stages, despite the existence of a national championship known as the Brier, social scientists remained puzzled by the strange things men were caught doing with their brooms.

According to one scientific observer, "Every winter, more and more men, most of them perfectly normal-looking middle-aged businessmen, respected members of the community, get together in an alley of ice, to throw rocks at one another." Although it was widely assumed by such observers that curlers were nothing more than run-of-the-mill alcoholics who, in their drunken stupor, had imagined a new game to play, no one could say for sure which addiction took precedence: curling or drinking.

Despite such glaring uncertainties surrounding the epidemic of "throwing rocks and slugging Scotch," these early analysts did provide some compelling evidence about the typical habits of a man who has let himself go. In a report published by the "Canadian Centre for Curling Aficionados," the following symptoms were published and distributed to health centres across Canada:

"The first symptom of a man being masticated by the curling bug," the report began, "is his sudden interest in brooms. Just ordinary brooms. His wife, for instance, catches him one night, sneaking out the back door, with her broom under his coat. When she tries to make him tell her what he is going to do with the broom, he merely stares at her in grim silence, his eyes gleaming with the wild light of the fanatic."

According to industry data, however, this type of silent, brooding curler is not quite as common as the deceptive curler, who invents a scenario in a rather pathetic attempt to curry favour with the wife, a situation that is bound to backfire.

"Or the more cunning type of curler," the report also adds, "may take the broom out of the closet on the pretense of going out to clear the snow off the front porch. Then, as soon as he gets outside the house, a big black sedan, full of more men with brooms, skips to the curb, picks him up and roars away into the night. Some women have even suspected the old man of running around with a witch, until they found out he had become a curler, and shot themselves."

Suffice it to say, if you recognize such symptoms in a loved one, there is little you can do. Medical professionals now agree that the chance of a full-fledged curling addict making a full recovery is as slim as making a triple raise, angle double takeout with the game on the line. In other words, it's not going to happen.

Finally, for those whose loved ones are still struck by the curling bug but are valiantly trying to kick the habit, the best treatment is to let them listen to the sounds of the game. After all, aside from their profound love of brooms, most curlers are equally drawn to the roar of a rock gliding over pebbled ice, to the husky screams of a player berating the sweepers, or to the beauty of witty curling banter. For this reason, we now give you the best and strangest quotes the roaring game has elicited.

His hats, his hoods, his bones,
His allay bowles, and curling stones.
The sacred game to celebrat,
Which to the gods are consecrat.
—Henry Adamson,
17th-century Scottish reader

To curle on the ice, does greatly please,
Being a manly Scottish exercise;
It clears the Brains, stirs up the Native Heat,
And gives a gallant appetite for Meat.
—Dr. Alex Peneciuk,
18th-century Scottish poet

It is foolish to let the facts spoil a good story.
—Cactus Jack Wells

You're loved by one and all here, and the fact that you've got four hundred million dollars in the bank has nothing to do with it.
–Cactus Jack Wells, to Macdonald Tobacco CEO David M. Stewart, who sponsored the Brier until 1979

Choice of stones is almost as important as choice of a wife. It must not be done lightly or inadvisably.
–Reverend John Kerr, 19th-century chaplain of the Royal Grand Caledonian Curling Club

I'm a curling addict: I need a hit and I want to get stoned.
–Author unknown

…sweep the piss out of it!
–Eddie Werenich, during his championship run at the '83 Brier

I'm 65 going on 30. But this week I'm 105 because it's been a bad week.
–Shorty Jenkins, when asked about his age

A curling rock is smarter than a human being.
–Shorty Jenkins, whose ice-making mantra is that ice is smarter than people

First few nights of an event he sleeps in the machine room, right by the condenser. Shorty likes to listen to the hum of the machinery, get used to the sound and how hard the machines are working. Anything shuts off in the middle of the night, you lose a day's curling the next morning. Not Shorty. He may have been burned once when the power went out, but never again. You go into the engine room of an arena, you see bedsheets and a pillow right there on the floor, surrounded by machines. That's Shorty.

–George Karrys, Olympic silver medalist in 1998 and publisher of *The Curling News*

Bob Stewart always had an active hand in the menu selection for the [Scott Tournament of Hearts] *Victory Banquet. For years he had suggested beets, but I managed to ignore this (I hate beets). In 1988 (by now he was president of Scott paper) he insisted. However, we had a major challenge in moving 500 guests up a narrow staircase from the reception area to the ballroom. As a result, all the vegetables, including the beets, were burned and had to be replaced. I'll never forget Bob's remarks that night when he said, "I have been trying for years to get Robin to put beets on the menu. I have accomplished that. I still have to find a way to get her to put them on your plates." Ten years later, when he went in for surgery, I sent a beets bouquet to his hospital room.*

–Robin Wilson, Scott Tournament of Hearts co-ordinator

He was the McEnroe of curling. In the '70s, he'd travel in a VW van, partying and drinking beer. He always wore plaid pants. Rumour has it he never washed them.

–2000 World Champion Brent Pierce, recalling Paul Gowsell's heyday

I think the women are going to have to curl naked in order to get people out there. I'm not kidding. You're going to have to get Anna Kournikova to come along to really jazz things up.

–Colleen Jones, on women's curling after it was separated from the men's event at the World Championships

I don't know. It took me 25 years to take off my moustache.

–Randy Ferbey, when asked if he would pose for a nude men's curling calendar

Factspiel

Not long after Colleen Jones suggested that women might need to curl naked to attract fans, a calendar of nude female curlers was printed, featuring Austria's Claudia Toth on the cover. Colleen Jones, who wasn't in the calendar, had this to say: "I wasn't asked. Should I be insulted? Part of me wants to be outraged. But if this gets them the money to compete and generates some interest, I guess I'm for it."

I'd rather play for money than badges.
—Jeff Stoughton, on having to choose
between winning money on the World
Curling Tour and the purple-hearted
badge you get for winning the Brier

*Eat to win, eat to lose, I don't care as long as
I eat.*
—John Kawaja, making fun of the curling
book *Eat To Win*, which stresses diet as
a major factor in winning

*We're not into [staying in shape]. We see food,
we eat it. We see something to drink, we drink
it. Then we go to bed.*
—Ed Werenich, on his team's attitude to
staying in shape

Round mound of come-around.
—Neil Harrison, describing his former
teammate Paul Savage on Dean
Gemmell's *The Curling Show*

*I have a speech therapist who says I could lose
my voice permanently if I keep curling.*
—Russ Howard

Blood is thicker than screech.
—Russ Howard, on cheering for his brother
Glenn in the 2007 Brier final against Russ'
former Olympic teammate Brad Gushue
from Newfoundland

It's not just a rock. It's forty-two pounds of pol-
ished granite, with a beveled underbelly and
a handle a human being can hold. Okay, so in
and of itself it looks like it has no practical pur-
pose, but it's a repository of possibility. And, when
it's handled just right, it exacts a kind of poetry—
as close to poetry as I ever want to get. The way it
moves...Not once, in everything I've done, have I
ever felt the same wonder and humanity as when
I'm playing the game of curling.

> –Paul Gross, John Krizanc and Paul
> Quarrington, *Men with Brooms*

It was as though I had farted. They didn't
know where to look.

> –Paul Gross (director and star of *Men*
> *with Brooms*), on people's reaction
> when they learned he was making
> a film about curling

Curling is not a sport. I called my grandmother
and told her she could win a gold medal
because they have dusting in the Olym-
pics now.

> –Charles Barkley, former NBA star
> and basketball analyst

We'll explain the appeal of curling to you if you
explain the appeal of the National Rifle Asso-
ciation to us.

> –Andy Barrie, performing a Canadian
> address to Americans

Here I was, champion of a 'spiel held some place near Kitchener, hovering over my wife's bed holding a platter of T-bone steaks as my prize.

–amateur curler Jeff Imai, a Toronto lawyer, after winning a bonspiel in Uxbridge, Ontario

This year, I played Glenn Howard four or five times. I played Al Hackner. I played Guy Hemmings. We've been battling each other for 30 years now. It's like an old-folks home out there. There are no secrets–you play hard and you go to the bar.

–Ed Werenich, reflecting on the curling life towards the end of his career

He thinks he's God. He always will.

–David Nedohin, in reference to Kevin Martin

Typical Kevin. It couldn't be him. It had to be the rocks. It's always something else. It's never Kevin Martin.

–Marcel Rocque, telling a story about a Martin loss to Ferbey's team in *The Ferbey Four*

I don't dwell on anything much other than train hard and be ready for the next big event. I tend to delete a lot of stuff. That's the way I've always been. I'm not sure if it's good or otherwise. It's just the way I am.

–Kevin Martin

Curlers across the country are similar in nature. When you are inside the curling club you feel like you are home. You feel like people know you. It is a family thing. Not only the family in terms of playing with your dad and your kids. You go to different places and you feel like you know them too.
  –Guy Hemmings, in Scott Russell's book *Open House: Canada and the Magic of Curling*

You can't forget the grassroots of curling. If I could help the sport, that would be wonderful. The sport has been really good for me. I'm not talking money-wise, I'm talking personally. As an individual I have improved a lot by playing this game. If I can help kids discover the same path that I discovered sixteen years ago then I will be proud of myself.
  –Guy Hemmings, in *Open House*

Chapter Five

Sticks and Stones

The curling rink is where town and country meet. Since curling's advent, people have been meeting at the curling rink because it's a place to socialize, to throw a few stones, to compete with friends and family, to share a few laughs and to hear the local gossip while having a drink.

Back in the day, of course, the curling club was an old boys' club, and there are certainly still some clubs around that retain their patriarchal feel. But curling has become an incredibly diverse sport, in part because anyone can pick up a stone and huck it down a sheet of ice. This simple fact has allowed curling to evolve into an inclusive game that appeals to anyone with a pulse. Having said that, it is a sport of great finesse, technique and, increasingly, raw power.

It is also relatively recent that curling has moved into the heavy-duty television era in which advertising dollars and big league revenues work as primary driving forces. Despite this recent shift, curling is quite clearly in a different financial ballpark than mainstream sports such as hockey, basketball, baseball and football. And being in the second tier certainly has its advantages, especially at the communal level.

Locked as we are, however, in a high-stakes sporting era in which the "for the love of the game" cliché has been drained of all meaning by money, mainstream media and corporate sponsorship, it is heart-warming to know that curling remains intimately tied to its roots. Of course, most Canadian cities and towns also have hockey rinks where kids can play without getting wrapped up in dreams of being a wealthy star, but that doesn't last long. Money is now intricately tied to hockey, basketball, baseball and football in a way that the innocence of childhood fantasies can ignore for only so long.

When I was growing up in the '80s, it was still possible to imagine being Gretzky during a game of shinny without thinking for a split-second about money. But now? Is it possible for teenagers to imagine being Sidney Crosby without dreaming of dollar figures, while having images of Nike symbols dancing in their heads?

In the curling world, on the other hand, the financial scale is considerably smaller and more local. Sure, there are increasing levels of corporate involvement, and the new Grand Slam format created by the World Curling Tour has ensured that a few teams will make a pretty decent whack of cash. But even top-flight curlers like Randy Ferbey and Kevin Martin hold down day jobs.

On the community scale, and at the amateur level, there is no curling industry in which coaches, parents or scouts conspire to whip kids into shape on the off-chance that they're good enough to hit the jackpot like they could by making the NHL. As a result, it is still feasible for a couple of homers to discover during their 20s that they have a curling knack and so form a foursome based on the good old-fashioned qualities of camaraderie and chemistry. After that, who knows. The world, as they say, is your oyster. And in the curling world, where provincial playdowns allow any old club-level team to compete, a group of curling hacks could get lucky at a bonspiel or two and start feeling good about their chances of giving The Old Bear (Kevin Martin) a run for his money should the stars align.

More important, though, is that the social gulf between Randy Ferbey and the common fan is not insurmountable. Ferbey doesn't need bodyguards and security escorts when he shows up in Vernon for a bonspiel. And if you get lucky and run into Ferbey in the curling club after the game, you'd probably just talk to him instead of grovelling like a giddy teenager, as you would if Sidney Crosby bumped into you.

With all that in mind, it's time to spin a few yarns while shedding some light on the glory of the game.

The Eight End That Wasn't

In bowling, a perfect game consists of 12 strikes and a score of 300. In curling, a perfect end is when all eight stones your team throws score a point. In curling lingo, it's called an eight-ender, and it is an extremely rare occurrence. But when Ken Watson was the curling kingpin back in the 1930s, he once "came within a cigar ash of the eight end."

As Watson himself explained, it was quite literally a long tube of cigar ash that got between his team and the coveted perfect end. This is how he described the shot:

"Johnny Buss (of the *Winnipeg Free Press*) gave Charlie Kerr a new cigar for the game and told him the way you smoked a cigar was to let the ash grow as long as possible. Well, when I threw my first rock, we were lying six and while Charlie was sweeping that stone, the cigar ash fell off right in front of the rock, and it ground to a halt just a foot or so from the rings. When I put my second stone in, we had the third seven end in Brier history. But we would have had the first eight end if it hadn't been for that darn cigar."

Factspiel

Ken Watson, who had the misfortune of having his legacy interrupted by World War II, still managed to win three national titles. On top of his curling prowess, however, he will forever be remembered as an innovator for revolutionizing the game with his infamous "Watson Slide." Watson was the first curler to push himself out of the hack and glide forward before releasing his stone.

The Mayflower Morgue

On the night of April 14, 1912, the RMS *Titanic* struck a monstrous iceberg off the southern coast of Newfoundland and began to sink. Two hours and 40 minutes later, the largest passenger steamship in the world went down for the count, carrying 1517 wealthy vacationers to their deaths.

In the ensuing aftermath, four ships were sent out of Halifax Harbour to retrieve the dead. After a feverish Maritime rescue effort, 333 bodies were recovered, and although some of the more badly decomposed corpses were buried at sea, most of them were sent to Halifax for identification. During the furor in Halifax, someone had the bright idea to use the old Mayflower Curling Club on Agricola Street as a temporary morgue. The bodies could be put on ice while John Henry Barnstead, Halifax's Deputy Registrar of Deaths, worked at identifying them.

In the end, most of the bodies were buried in cemeteries throughout Halifax, while many of their personal effects and recovered *Titanic* artifacts are still housed in either the Maritime Museum of the Atlantic or the Public Archives of Nova Scotia. The Mayflower, for its part, is still going strong, though its location changed in 1961, when it was moved from Agricola Street (now an army surplus store) to its current location on Monaghan Drive.

The Leslie Wells Chorale

As detailed by legendary Canadian broadcaster and media personality "Cactus" Jack Wells in an essay he wrote for *The First Fifty: A Nostalgic Look at the Brier,* the Leslie Wells Singers were formed in an impromptu fashion when a bunch of media hacks got drunk. It happened in Sudbury, during the 1953 Brier.

Cactus Jack's story is that the group banded together in song after lamenting the newly minted tradition of singing the national anthem at sporting events. According to Wells, most fans sang along to "O Canada" with "as much enthusiasm as a guy going to the electric chair." To combat the repeated exposure to such spiritless scenes, Wells formed the Leslie Wells Singers, whose original members included Easy Ed McAuley, Annis Stukus, Maurice Smith, Johnny Esaw, Frank O'Brien, Reg Geary, Scotty Melville, Scott Harper and Breathless Bill Good. In memoriam of their various achievements, Cactus Jack concluded that "over the past 50 years, if the Brier has produced anything of merit, it's the Leslie Wells Singers, a choral group of media men and hangers-on who make the Mormon Tabernacle Choir sound like a small boy scratching chalk on a blackboard."

Of course, like any drunken group of hoarse singers, they smoked like banshees and performed many foul-mouthed renditions of otherwise polite songs. Here, for example, are the lyrics to their classic number, which was sung to the tune of "Mary Had a Little Lamb":

Sudbury's a horseshit town, horseshit town,
horseshit town.
Sudbury's a horseshit town, we haven't been
laid today.
We haven't been laid today, we haven't been
laid today.
Sudbury's a horseshit town, horseshit town,
horseshit town.
Sudbury's a horseshit town, we haven't been
laid today.

And you thought curling crowds were polite and reserved. Shame on you!

"The Black Bonspiel of Wullie MacCrimmon"

If you like bad puns, you might just love "The Black Bonspiel of Wullie MacCrimmon." Originally written by W.O. Mitchell in 1951 as a radio play, and then adapted for television (in 1965) and the stage (first performed in 1979 by Theatre Calgary), it is a satirical play about curling.

Set in Wildrose, Alberta, in the 1930s, the play revolves around the conflict between a morality squad and the common people who just want to have fun. The story, being loosely Faustian, pits the Devil, a crusading local businessman who wants to ban curling on Sundays, against the local cobbler Wullie MacCrimmon. Wullie makes a deal with the devilish businessman in order to become a championship curler, and from there the puns come as fast and furious as when Ron MacLean has the spotlight. Despite its hokiness, the play doesn't pretend to be classic Shakespearean theatre. Instead, it basks in its own silliness, with beauty lines such as "Macbeth shall sweep no more!"

The Carspiel

In the early '80s, when Ontario's Eddie Werenich stepped into the national spotlight by winning the Brier in 1983, his so-called Dream Team consisted of an exciting combination of youthful power and savvy yet aggressive veterans. The veterans were Werenich and his long-time teammate Paul Savage. The youth consisted of Neil Harrison on the front end, and John Kawaja, a hip-looking upstart and one of the game's original power seconds, who could really bust up the house if things got hairy.

Kawaja, who now works in the golfing industry (another great Scottish invention) for Adidas/Taylor-Made, was recently interviewed by Dean Gemmell on *The Curling Show*. One of Kawaja's stories about his curling glory days took place in Vernon, BC, where his team was in town in 1982 for a carspiel, which they won.

Their prize was four Pontiac Acadians, which they sold to local residents during the day. Of course, because his team owned the cars for such a brief time, Kawaja couldn't be sure the cars were in fact Acadians, but he did recall selling the first two for $5000 a piece, the third for $4500, and the last one, because they'd been drinking at the local watering hole for a little too long, for the friendly sum of $4000.

The Battle of the Sexes

The idea behind a curling "Battle of the Sexes" originated in the tennis world. In September 1973, tennis showman Bobby Riggs challenged Billie Jean King to a "Battle of the Sexes." Before the match against King, however, Riggs had already thrust himself into the public eye by challenging and beating the number one female tennis player in a Mother's Day match earlier in the year. After mopping the court with Margaret Court by scores of 6–2 and 6–1, Riggs made the cover of *Sports Illustrated* and *Time* and went on to taunt female tennis players for their collective inferiority. Riggs, you see, was 55 years old at the time, and his heyday had been 30 years earlier, in the 1940s. King, on the other hand, was at the peak of her tennis career and the number one ranked female tennis player.

In any case, when the time came for the Riggs-King showdown, which was televised nationally in the U.S. on September 20, King entered the Astrodome in Houston à la Cleopatra, carried in a gold litter held aloft by four bare-chested studs dressed as ancient slaves. For his part, Riggs followed King into the stadium in a rickshaw that was drawn by a harem of scantily clad models, whom he dubbed "Bobby's Bosom Buddies."

When the match started, however, it was clear that King had a strategy, and this time it was a woman who put Riggs in his place. Believing that "it would set [women] back 50 years if I didn't win," King pummelled Riggs 6–4, 6–3, 6–3. Instead of negatively impacting women's self-esteem as she had feared, King's victory over Riggs galvanized women in sports in a way that her six Wimbledon titles and four U.S. Open victories never did.

On the heels of this tennis tête-à-tête, the reigning world curling champion Orest Meleschuk was challenged to a "Battle of the Sexes" match by the reigning Canadian women's champion Vera Pezer. As it turned out, the match was a big event that was broadcast nationally by CBC, marking the first time women's curling had been showcased on network television. Of course, it was widely assumed that The Big O (Orest Meleschuk) would sweep Pezer away. But it didn't play out that way.

In front of his home fans in Manitoba's St. James Arena, Meleschuk curled poorly, and Pezer's Saskatchewan rink easily won the game. But Pezer was unimpressed with The Big O's lackadaisical approach to the game: "He didn't take us seriously," she said. "At a press conference before the game, he asked us if we played takeouts or just draws. He curled poorly. All it meant is we could beat a hungover male skip."

Still, it was the first "Battle of the Sexes" in curling history, and it set a precedent. It may not have raised curling's profile in the way the tennis match between King and Riggs raised tennis' profile, but a little over a decade later, two of curling's most colourful characters, Ed Werenich and Marilyn Bodogh, would take care of that.

The Spectacle of the Sexes

The year was 1986. Marilyn Bodogh and Eddie Werenich were in their heyday, both as players and as personalities. Neither Marilyn nor Eddie minced words; they shot from the hip and weren't afraid of the spotlight. So when they stepped onto the stage on a Friday night in Toronto during the 1986 World Championships, they turned "The Battle of the Sexes" into a spectacle of excess.

For starters, The Wrench, as Eddie was dubbed, entered the arena wearing a silk robe and crown as the tune from *Rocky* belted out of the loud-speakers. Then came Marilyn in her trademark kilt. And what did she do but a cartwheel. The crowd went ballistic. Of course, it should be mentioned that the game stunk, and Marilyn Bodogh's rink got plastered by the Rocky-inspired Wrench. But it didn't matter. Everyone had a whale of a time.

Oh, and then there was the after-party in downtown Toronto at the Royal Canadian Curling Club. According to some curling buff named Stuart who claims he was a member of the Royals in '86, there were so many people in the club that the upstairs viewing area and its ballroom dance floor were packed to the gills, while downstairs, people were crammed onto the six sheets of ice like canned sardines.

To this day, the aftermath of the most notorious "Battle of the Sexes" set a gross bar revenue record that still hasn't been matched. So put that in your pipe and smoke it!

The Streaker

When it comes to sports streaking, there is one man who has made a name for himself. His name is The Streaker. He has even had it trademarked.

But The Streaker's real name is Mark Roberts. He is a Liverpool resident who has a wicked, self-deprecating sense of humour, and over the past few years, Roberts has exposed his dangling junk for such sports as rugby, soccer, tennis, football, pool, golf and, last but not least, curling.

At the 2006 Winter Olympics in Torino, during a riveting round-robin curling confrontation between Scotland and the United States, The Streaker came down to ice level wearing a diaper on his head and a plastic chicken secured with packing tape over his "package." An unemployed father of three, Roberts has been streaking since 1993, at which time he interrupted a Rugby Sevens match in Hong Kong.

In an interview for *Real Sports with Bryant Gumbel*, Roberts was asked what was wrong with him. "What's the matter with me?" he laughed. "Well, if making millions and millions of people laugh by taking me clothes off, if there's a fault in that, well, I think there's something wrong with the world. At the end of the day, humour is the only thing that makes the world go round." Then, when asked whether the world really needs to see his self-described "wobbly body," he had this to say: "If I had a lovely body, and I was very well-endowed, people would call me a poser. But I'm not. I've got a beer belly. I've got a big, wobbly fat ass, and I'm not very well-built downstairs either. So I think it adds to the humour." Right you are, Mark. Right you are.

Hurry Hard

"Hurry! Hard!" It is the notorious call of the wild on the curling sheet. And more than anyone else, Russ Howard has patented the call, making it both a subject to copy for those new to the game and to ridicule for those outside observers who find themselves bemused by the Canadian nuances that shape most curling rituals.

In Danish, the call translates as "Hurtig! Hardt," and Ulrick Schmidt is the kingpin of the intense scream. But one of the more popular translations among fans is the Russian version, which roughly means "More!" and sounds something like "Eshow!" Perhaps worried that his trademark call was catching on and that he might lose his patented "Hurry! Hard!," Howard recently co-authored a book with the legendary curling journalist Bob Weeks, called, you guessed it, *Hurry Hard: The Russ Howard Story.*

Asham World Curling Tour

The Asham World Curling Tour (WCT) is a relative newcomer to the curling world, but like the PGA Tour in golf and the ATP Tour in tennis, it is a money tour that now boasts four Grand Slam events throughout the year. Created in 1992, the WCT is a group of curling bonspiels for men. The four Grand Slam events each feature $100,000 purses, and they all take place on Canadian soil. The BDO Canadian Classic takes place in Québec City in November; then, at the end of December, The National is hosted by Port Hawkesbury, Nova Scotia; in the new year, the Masters of Curling takes place in Regina at the end of January; and finally, at the end of the curling season, the Tylenol Players' Championship is hosted by St. John's, Newfoundland, in late April.

The WCT, however, has been controversial since its inception. Rooted in player dissatisfaction with the direction the Canadian Curling Association (CCA) was taking, the WCT was founded by a group of curlers and advertisers who included the likes of Ed Lukowich, Ray Turnbull, James Furgale and Arnold Asham. Although most players supported the tour and its players' association (the World Curling Players' Association), things came to a head in 2001 and 2002, when Kevin Martin spearheaded a boycott of the Brier, leaving all Canadian curlers with a nasty ultimatum: either boycott the Brier or be banned from the WCT. In the end, the dispute fractured curlers into two camps.

Many high-profile curlers such as Martin, Wayne Middaugh, Jeff Stoughton and Kerry Burtnyk chose to boycott the Brier by signing exclusivity deals in 2001 with the WCT. According to David Nedohin, however, who shoots last on the Randy Ferbey team that chose to stand by the Brier, banning players from the WCT just because they wanted to honour the Brier is where Martin and his cohorts crossed the line. According to Nedohin, "Our team, for our own reasons, did not agree with the boycott, especially given that we had 24 hours to make our decision. As much as we supported the initiative of the players' association fully to build the tour and attempt to win extra bonuses from the Canadian Curling Association at the Brier, we did not agree with the method at the time.

"This was where Kevin [Martin] crossed the line, in my mind. He was the leader in an initiative to have us banned from the tour completely. Our team had wholeheartedly supported and continued to support the tour. However, the 'decision' was no longer in our hands as we were given an ultimatum. Kevin continued to insist we turned our backs on the players when we were the ones who were being shunned."

Sure enough, after choosing to play in the 2002 Brier playdowns, Randy Ferbey and his team were banned from the WCT for three years. It must have felt as though they were being stone-walled. Since then, they've had their accomplishments consistently diminished because many high-calibre teams weren't competing in the Brier. On the other hand, boycotting the Brier to stick it to the CCA must have seemed a little beyond the pale.

One of the key mediators in the dispute turned out to be former NHL defenseman and Stanley Cup champion Paul Boutilier. Hired in 2002 as the head of the WCT and the World Curling Players' Association, Boutilier was brought in to deal with a tense and messy situation. Although he recently stepped down from both positions, Boutilier was instrumental in setting up a system whereby all players could compete in the WCT Grand Slams, while also being free to compete in provincial playdowns en route to the Brier. Finally, with TSN having the rights to broadcast the Brier and the Tournament of Hearts, one of Boutilier's last initiatives was to negotiate an eight-year deal with the CBC to broadcast the lucrative Grand Slam events.

Of course, throughout the kerfuffle, the WCT was trying to establish itself while improving its bargaining position with the CCA-led Brier so that the two curling bodies could negotiate from positions of relative equality. And since the boycott of 2002, the existence of the Grand Slam events has certainly helped raise the stakes in curling across the board. Today, not only are all players able to compete in WCT events, but the dispute helped spur the CCA to create cash incentives for Brier accomplishments.

Finally, if you put any stock in recent rumours, there seems to be a good chance another Grand Slam event in the lucrative American market will be created within the next few years. And if that happens, well, curling might well be on its way to seeing sponsorship dollars that even this generation of curlers has only dreamed of.

The Canadian Curling Association

The Canadian Curling Association (CCA) has been Canadian curling's official governing body since it was originally formed as the Dominion Curling Association in 1935. But for much of its recent history, it has been under heavy scrutiny. Things started getting messy in 1987 when the CCA informed Ed Werenich and Paul Savage that they would have to shed a few pounds if they wanted to represent Canada at the Olympics. Werenich was particularly outraged by the public embarrassment that ensued, and the war of words between The Wrench and the CCA has continued ever since.

In 1990, when Werenich won his second Brier, he threatened to boycott the World Championship unless the CCA-appointed national coach stayed behind.

He and Savage then hired a stripper named Marina to be their coach at the Olympic Trials as a means of mocking the CCA and their CCA-appointed national coach. Although the stripper never made a curling-related appearance, it's easy to understand why Werenich never got along with CCA bigwigs like Dave Parkes and Warren Hansen.

But these personality clashes and petty hostilities were nothing compared to what took place in 2001 and 2002 when many disgruntled players banded together to challenge the supremacy of the CCA. Or perhaps Werenich's battles served as precursors. In any case, much like the advent of the World Hockey Association (WHA) in 1972, which divided the hockey world for several years, the Asham World Curling Tour briefly fractured the game by attracting some of the best players to its money tour. Any way you slice it though, the tour makes good sense for the game of curling. It's just too bad it had to grow out of increasing resentment towards the CCA.

One of the central reasons for the contentious split was a general dissatisfaction on the part of

Delivering a solid curling shot requires three props: the hack, into which the player plants his feet and pushes off; the stone, the bottom of which should be clean; and the broom, which is held in the off-hand and used for balance while gliding out of the hack and toward the hog line.

the players, who were tired of seeing the Brier generate lucrative revenue, only to see the bulk of it going to the CCA instead of to the players. In essence, 2001–02 was curling's labour dispute, and although it threatened the future of curling, the issue was resolved by the end of 2002, and today the game's best players can play in both CCA events and WCT events, without having to choose sides.

But let's get back to Dave Parkes for a minute. Before resigning in 2007, he had been the CCA's CEO since 1988, and his 19-year run saw many changes in the world of curling. For starters, Parkes helped steer curling into the television era by staging the Brier in large arenas. Inaugurated in 1994, the so-called Season of Champions boosted the sport's image, while also bringing in greater revenues. With increased revenues, however, came increased demand from the players for a larger cut of the profits. Ultimately, the Brier's financial success is what caused the post-millennium tension and, almost inevitably, the advent of the World Curling Tour.

But more recently, Parkes has made some bizarre decisions that have affected the CCA's bottom line. His first decision was to move the Brier and the Tournament of Hearts from TSN to a CBC digital channel that wasn't included in most basic cable packages. Quite naturally, curling fans across the country went nuts and flooded the CCA with complaints. So Parkes walked away from the CBC contract, which brought on lawsuits and huge legal bills. Taken all together, these decisions were financially disastrous for the CCA.

Finally, in 2007, Parkes stepped down from his post and was replaced by Greg Stremlaw. While it is difficult to gauge how this change may affect the future of the game, suffice it to say that the CCA is currently undergoing a major philosophical and fiscal overhaul. Nevertheless, the early returns seem positive. After one year in office, Stremlaw has overseen a fiscal shift of seismic proportions. In 2006–07, before Stremlaw took office, the CCA posted a $1.37-million deficit, but in 2008, the Ottawa-based organization posted a $1.4-million surplus, allowing it to pay off its debt and to begin its first-ever financial reserve fund.

The Continental Cup

Since 2002, The Continental Cup has been a joint venture between the Canadian Curling Association and its global partner, the World Curling Association. Although most curlers seem to find it a fun and unique event to participate in, its complicated format has yet to make for compelling television. In effect, it is curling's version of the Ryder Cup in golf in that it is a two-team competition: Team North America vs. Team World.

The competition takes place over four days and features both men and women in various team games, including mixed doubles, singles and skins games. Although the scoring system is too complex to briefly summarize, let's just say that without a straightforward scoring system, the Continental Cup will continue to have trouble attracting new and even dedicated curling fans to its event.

The Skins Game

A curling skins game is similar to a golf or bowling skins game that uses a points system from end to end. In essence, this means that each end takes on heightened importance by pitting four invited players against each other with cold hard cash on the line. TSN, which had produced and televised the skins events from 1986 to 2004, brought back the popular event in 2007 with a total cash purse of $100,000.

An exciting event that takes place over a weekend, a skins game consists of four hand-picked teams who each play in an eight-end semi-final. With each end worth a dollar amount that increases as the game goes on, the winning team is the one that pockets the most cash. Significantly, the way to win an end is to score two if you have the hammer, or to steal the end with at least one point if you don't. Otherwise, the money is carried over to the next end.

China Rising

At the 2008 World Women's Championships in Vernon, BC, Team China shocked the competition by being good curlers. Although Bingyu (Betty) Wang's team of young upstarts ultimately lost to Jennifer Jones and her powerhouse team, Wang played the underdog role to perfection, making it difficult not to cheer for her. Full of exuberance and enthusiasm, Wang and her teammates surprised the Canadians 9–7 in their round-robin game, although when push came to shove in the final, Canada came out on top by the score of 7–4.

Despite the final loss, China was the tournament's dominant team. After finishing the round-robin in first place, they went on to humble Canada a second time in the playoff round. But Canada won their next game, which set up a third meeting—this time in the final—between Canada and China.

Nevertheless, Wang's team is clearly a team to be reckoned with in the future. As recently as three years ago, Wang practiced on ice meant for hockey, because there wasn't a single curling rink in China. But in 2005, the first rink was built in Beijing. Despite the lack of facilities, the Chinese team has shown drastic improvement over a brief period. Prior to 2005, no Asian country had ever competed in a curling World Championship. That year, however, Wang's team qualified for the tournament in Scotland.

Although the Chinese men have yet to make a breakthrough of similar proportions, they are certainly making some noise. In the 2008 World Championships, Kevin Martin's rink dominated the round-robin part of the competition, finishing with an impressive 10–1 mark. Then, in the play-off round, Martin won gold for the first time at the Worlds. Despite his success, however, his one loss came to Fengchun Wang, whose Chinese team finished fourth in the tournament. The fourth place finish is, of course, an astonishing achievement given the fact that China has just over 100 curlers among its 1.3 billion citizens. And since the Chinese men have started practicing in Edmonton at the same club as Kevin Martin, the curling guru has noticed the consistency of his new adversary. "They are like machines. They do not miss many shots at all." Colleen Jones, another Canadian curling legend, echoed Martin's simile. "This is a wake-up call for Canada," she said recently from her home in Halifax. "The Chinese and Japanese, they curl like machines. It's hard to believe they ever miss."

The Calendar

In 2005, Spanish skip Ana Arce, who also works as a photographer, decided it was high time to dispel the idea that female curlers are all a bunch of stodgy old housewives. Okay, maybe that's going too far, but the idea of a curling calendar featuring nude or scantily clad female curlers was designed to generate a little revenue while also increasing the game's profile. The Ana Arce Sponsorship Calendar was produced in

2006 and 2007, each issue featuring female curlers from around the world.

Now, since that initial calendar came out, many have speculated that Colleen Jones played a role in generating Arce's idea. After all, it was Jones who once suggested that women would have to start curling naked to attract fans after the women's World Championship was separated from the men's. But I don't know. With a last name like "Arce," it's pretty much written in stone that you're going to be a show-off.

Rockstar Curling

Well, 2009 may be the year that curling goes big-time. With the 2010 Olympics taking place in Vancouver, the mainstream American network NBC has the rights to a reality TV show called *Rockstar Curling*. Like most reality TV, *Rockstar Curling* will provide everyday people with the chance to fulfill their dreams. Of course, it may be true that few Americans dream of curling glory, but a great number of Americans do dream of being Olympians, so why not use curling as the vehicle? At least that's the thinking behind *Rockstar Curling*.

The first step is to have nationwide tryouts all across America throughout 2008. Then, a panel of curling coaches will select two teams—five women and five men—who will spend six months training with coaches in Lake Placid, New York. After their rigorous training, both teams will then participate in the high-stakes U.S. Olympic Team Trials, which will provide them with the opportunity, remote though it may be, of going to the Olympics to represent the United States.

As for the TV show, it will of course heavily edit the tryouts, the training and the competitions to pare it all down into nine 30-minute weekly episodes, to be followed by an hour-long season finale. It's just too bad we won't get to see a bunch of washed-up rockstars like Axl Rose and Huey Lewis trying their hand at curling.

Chapter Six

Classic Curling Characters

It has been said that curling is a game of skill, strategy and sportsmanship. As a game, it has been compared to chess, shuffleboard, pool, *pétanque* and bocce. Of course, it has affinities with all of these games, mostly because all of them value the mind's finesse over the body's. Indeed, despite the new trend of curlers who take themselves a little too seriously by hitting the gym and refusing alcohol after a tightly contested match, having a vivid imagination is usually more important than being built like a brick outhouse.

As a result of the role intelligence and imagination play, curling has an illustrious history of bland stars who were brilliant tacticians. But blandness hasn't always been an impediment to curling's success. In many parts of Canada, and especially in the prairie provinces of Alberta, Saskatchewan and Manitoba, curling strategy comes to some children as naturally as language. In other places, however, curling can be downright puzzling to the observer. Why, for instance, do men and women think it perfectly normal to furiously sweep an already clean sheet of ice while another member of the team roars at the sweeper to "Hurry! Haaarrrd!"? While this may prove difficult to answer, there is no question that the use of such silly props helps attract some killer characters.

It could also be said that curling is the "everyman's" game. Until recently, no curlers could afford to curl full time, which meant that your typical curling star was a farmer or a firefighter, a teacher or a salesperson. And this is part of curling's appeal. At the highest level, curlers are regular men and women who are trying to juggle family and work, just like everyone else.

Finally, as Dean Gemmell, the sharp host of *The Curling Show*, has said on a number of occasions, despite some marketing advances, the curling world has generally failed to promote its legends in a way that is accessible to the modern fan. Moreover, Gemmell has also pointed out that the true uniqueness of curling lies in its strategy and conversation. This, after all, is where we get to think alongside the curlers we're watching, while analyzing their strategy and listening to their curious banter. With that in mind, let's take a look at some of the more memorable legends and priceless characters to have graced a curling sheet over the years.

Ken Watson (1904–86)

By all accounts, Ken Watson was the first curling star in the sport's history. Part of the reason for his stardom during the Depression era of the 1930s is what still makes Ken Watson's legacy relevant to today's game. Quite simply, prior to Watson's arrival, curling was a geriatric sport.

Of course, curling still has a relatively old demographic. But when Watson burst onto the scene as a young whippersnapper in his early 30s,

Showing off their old school brooms, this Gore Bay foursome display their Victorian stylings.

his competition was almost exclusively in their 50s and 60s. The game was dull and featured little imagination. By contrast, Watson was an innovator who wasn't afraid to upset the status quo. Of course, his greatest legacy was in bringing the Watson Slide into the game.

Prior to the Watson Slide, curlers basically stood in the hack, planted a foot in front of them and released their stone. Watson, on the other hand, was young and imaginative enough to pull off what must have seemed an incredibly athletic manoeuvre by pushing out of the hack and gracefully gliding along the ice before releasing his rock. Naturally, the old guard didn't look too fondly on this new move. "The Winnipeg Slide," as it was then called, was seen as a cheap move that gave Watson the advantage of releasing his rock a few feet closer to the house than his competition, stuck as they were back in the hack.

Despite the controversy his new move initially caused, there was no reason to ban the manoeuvre. Curling, we must remember, used to be an unofficiated sport that relied on etiquette and convention rather than hard-and-fast rules. This is of course changing as the stakes have risen with the introduction of money and the Olympics to the modern game. But in the period just prior to World War II, other than hearing a few early grumblings of moral objection, there was nothing to stop Watson from revolutionizing the game. And when anything relies on convention, it takes bold men or women to move things forward to prevent the apathy of the masses from taking root and getting too comfortable. This is what Ken Watson did.

Not only did Watson's relative youth and athleticism change the way the game was played, but his style and grace also made curling more attractive to younger audiences. Of course, in the pre-war era, there was little media coverage of curling. But Watson "modernized" the sport's image through his own image. He also had substance in addition to style. The man from Manitoba won three Briers (in 1936, 1942 and 1949) at a time when the sport went from being small potatoes to a big-time national spectacle. And although he wasn't alone, Watson helped usher in a new era of curling in which the game became a beautiful sport to watch.

Beyond his on-ice contributions, Watson was also one of the first real ambassadors of the game. He was a tireless promoter and teacher of the game, and his contributions were spread between the grassroots level and the more mainstream world of the media. As a high school teacher in Winnipeg, where he spent 20 years of his life, he built the first schoolboy curling program, a program that has worked its way into many high schools across Canada. During his years as a teacher, Watson also found time to write a great number of instructional articles for newspapers, not to mention four books. Most significantly, his book *Ken Watson on Curling*, which was published in 1950, was long seen as curling's bible for young curlers.

Although the book is somewhat outdated today as a result of the many changes in strategy and equipment, there is little doubt that Ken Watson would see the obsolescence of his book as a good thing for the game. After all, he introduced the curling world to the possibility of change, and the last thing he would want is to see curling stagnate, unable to balance tradition with modern demands.

Matt Baldwin (b. 1926)

It is a rare thing to see Matt Baldwin without a smile on his face. After Ken Watson had popularized curling by merging greatness with playfulness, Baldwin entered the stage in the early '50s and took showmanship to new heights.

To get away with showmanship, however, you have to be a good curler, otherwise you're only an attention junkie who hot dogs without a sense of purpose. But Baldwin was no hot dog. Rather, he was an entertainer who was aware of his audience and was just as good at winning championships as he was at telling a joke or pulling off a spontaneous prank. Indeed, Baldwin's techniques usually psyched out his opponents more than anything, as it was often easy to assume that Baldwin wasn't taking the game seriously.

Matt Baldwin, though, was the dominant curler of the late '50s. By winning Briers in 1954, 1957 and 1958, he was the curling hotshot before Ernie Richardson and his band of brothers came along in 1959 and blew the competition out of the water. But while Baldwin was in the limelight, he won, and he had fun, which was what brought him to curling in the first place. As he put it: "I figured it was a hell of a sport. Four guys can get together and drink, play cards and have a great time. I figured it was too good for the old guys."

Early in his career, while playing in Toronto at the Tournament of Champions, Baldwin began carving out his place in curling lore by trumping the infamous Watson Slide with his Baldwin Slide, an extended version of the slide Ken Watson had used to revolutionize the sport. After pushing out of the hack with maximum force, Baldwin slid halfway down the ice before casually taking his hand off the rock, scratching his nose, then grabbing the handle again. He continued all the way into the house, where he stopped and placed the rock on the button.

Then, in 1954, with the Brier being held in his own backyard of Edmonton, Baldwin gave in to his fans' repeated chants of "Slide! Slide!" Although he ignored the chants for a while, he eventually complied in the final game of the round-robin championship, when things were well in hand. He slid halfway down the ice before releasing his stone, and wouldn't you know it, his shot landed plum on the button. "It was the flukiest shot of my life," he later said, "but everyone seemed to like it."

This was the beginning of his career, and towards its tail end, Baldwin proved he hadn't lost his sense of humour, even if he wasn't the same dominant curler he had been in the late '50s. The year was 1971, and the Brier was in Québec City. With a snowstorm raging outside, the power suddenly shut off, leaving the arena in total darkness. Between trips to the darkened bar, Baldwin and his team furtively arranged all of their eight stones around the 4-foot, so that when the lights eventually came back on, the Baldwin team was gone, but they had the perfect 8-ender set up. After the initial shock and confusion of both fans and the opposition, Baldwin and his teammates calmly strolled out of the bar to roars of approval from the fans.

Ernie Richardson (b. 1931)

In many ways, Ernie Richardson is the quintessential old school curler. Born in Stoughton, Saskatchewan, in 1931, Ernie grew up on the Prairies and demonstrated a regal mien as a curler, a businessman and a family man. Big Ern, as he was affectionately dubbed, was a strapping man who never looked fazed by pressure, and as his successes mounted, he became, quite simply, The King. Of course, The King's heyday was between 1959 and 1963, when he won four Briers and four Scotch Cups in a five-year span.

But unlike his namesake Elvis Presley, The King was no one-man show. Indeed, Ernie Richardson's curling saga is a family affair. There was his cousin Wes, who shot lead; his brother Garnet (known throughout his career as Sam), who shot second; and at third was Arnold, another cousin. And rounding out the troops was Ernie.

Collectively, the Richardsons' greatness forced the game to grow; when the group came on the scene, the curling world had never seen anything as cohesive, nor as consistent. According to *Globe and Mail* columnist and curling aficionado Bob Weeks, "What Arnold Palmer is to golf and what

Gordie Howe is to hockey, the Richardsons are to curling." Interestingly, Weeks does not single Ernie out, and no doubt this has both to do with the nature of curling and the unprecedented chemistry the Richardsons displayed in their triumphs.

Despite the teamwork, it must also be said that Big Ern's team won because they had The King. As a star and a skip, he was a clutch shot-maker and as humble as apple pie. After five years of trail-blazing success, the Richardsons stepped out of the limelight and went their separate ways. When the dust settled, Ernie opened a lighting company in Regina called Richardson House of Fixtures and Supplies. In 1979, a second store was opened in Saskatoon, and the family business, now called Richardson Lighting, continues to thrive.

Cactus Jack Wells (1911–99)

Cactus Jack Wells was born in Moose Jaw, Saskatchewan, but he bled Bomber blue and was the first voice of the Brier. Relying on a booming voice and a relentless wit, Cactus Jack was curling's entertainer, its emcee and its social leader for the better part of 30 years.

Before we get to his impact on curling, though, Cactus Jack was one of those larger-than-life media personalities who, like Howard Cosell, transcended the often insular sports world with the scope of his commentary. As the voice of the Brier and of the Winnipeg Blue Bombers, Cactus Jack was quick-witted and discerning, even if he couldn't be bothered trying to pronounce players' names accurately. But to Cactus Jack, the names weren't all that important. Rather, it was important to keep fans entertained. Known for his hideous sports jackets and a raspy, distinctive voice, Cactus Jack liked to laugh, and he liked to make people laugh.

In some ways, Cactus Jack was like Don Cherry, what with the loud suits, the inability (or unwillingness) to pronounce names accurately, and the irrepressible opinions. But Cactus Jack was a more diverse broadcaster than Cherry is, and a more accurate comparison may be to Harry Caray or to Howard Cosell. Like Cosell, Cactus Jack made the broadcast "bigger than the game." And like Caray, Cactus Jack was a little wild, and he never really retired. Instead, he just kept calling Winnipeg Blue Bomber games until death came and took him away.

At the curling rink, Cactus Jack played the field like he was Bob Hope. During his countless years at the Brier, he formed the Leslie Wells Singers, a group of media men whose singing prowess became a Brier tradition—mostly because drinking, smoking and storytelling has always been an integral part of the joy of curling.

Another interesting aspect of Jack's career is that in the early 1950s, he turned down an offer to become the play-by-play voice for *Hockey Night in Canada*. While I haven't the slightest idea why he did so, it is a fact that the Brier format allowed him to socialize and interview fans and curlers in a way that being a hockey voice wouldn't have afforded. Moreover, curling is slow enough that it needs a great storyteller to avoid the onset of boredom. And this is what new curling fans don't understand. Curling has as much to do with yakking and chatting with your buddies as it has to do with the *action* unfolding on the ice. And because Cactus Jack could talk until the cows came home, he was perfect for the world of curling.

David M. Stewart (1920–84)

In the 1920s, when a man named George Cameron approached Walter M. Stewart, the head of Macdonald Tobacco, about setting up a national curling championship, Stewart thought it was such a capital idea that he committed to sponsoring the Brier. And for 50 years (1927–42 and 1946–79), Macdonald Tobacco did just that. The funny thing was that Stewart never attended a single Brier. According to his son David, who took over the company and became a very public Brier figure, Walter was an intensely shy man. Apparently, Walter also felt that a sponsor's role was not meant to be public. Instead, he believed a good sponsor helped the event flourish by providing a clear direction, which could in turn guide the people directly involved in organizing the event.

Like his father, David M. Stewart was a shy man, though you'd never know it from the clothes he wore. When presenting the Brier Tankard, Stewart was renowned for wearing a thick coonskin coat, not to mention a black handle-bar moustache. The flashy old-world look, though, was appropriate for a man of old-world refinement. In addition to running a tobacco company, Stewart was a humanist and a philanthropist who collected art (his collection is now held in Montréal's David M. Stewart Museum) and sponsored a wide variety of events and causes. According to the museum's website, Stewart believed that "it is fundamental to bring history to life, not merely exhibiting objects as a way of explaining a topic or an idea." Similarly, if curling is to grow as a sport while retaining its beautiful traditions, it is important to present the past in new and unique ways that don't just reek of being antique.

Shorty Jenkins (b. 1935)

Clarence "Shorty" Jenkins is about as iconic a figure as you could imagine for the curling world. An old man who is rarely seen without his trademark pink cowboy hat, Shorty is a hard-working dude with a knack for figuring things out. In other words, he represents the do-it-yourself school of yesteryear, where observation and common sense matter a whole lot more than experience and rigorous training.

And like so many curling legends, Shorty entered the curling world by chance and stayed because he found a talent he didn't know he had.

A former military man who rattled around the service for the better part of 10 years, Shorty quit the military in March 1967. Later that year, he found himself living in Trenton, Ontario, with his wife Johanna and their two young children. During a two-week vacation from his job managing a Sunoco gas station, Shorty decided to enter a golf tournament, likely, as he would put it, for the hell of it. Ever the opportunist, Shorty noticed the greenskeeper quitting during his round and so decided to seize the chance. That day, he was hired as the greenskeeper of the Trenton Golf and Curling Club.

As summer moved into fall, the club also lost its ice man for their curling rink, so Shorty applied, hoping to turn seasonal work into a year-round job. According to Shorty, though, he didn't get the job at first because he was seen as being "too hyper" for the diligent and vigilant task of maintaining consistent ice. Later on, when the position was officially posted, Shorty re-applied, only to be turned down again. But the club was in a fix, and Shorty knew it. With curling season looming, and no other applicants, Shorty finally talked his way into the position by promising to quit if Harold Hemstead, the club's owner, ever took issue with Shorty's work. Apparently, that never happened.

Given the challenge of proving his mettle to a man who didn't believe in him, Shorty did some homework before curling season. By the time he had to lay his first sheet of ice, he had driven all around Ontario, soliciting strategies and technical advice from other ice makers. Soon enough, Shorty got the hang of it, and his employer never grumbled much. But after hearing a few rumblings from some of the club's players that the ice was playing at different speeds from day to day, Shorty investigated. Knowing *he* hadn't done anything differently, Shorty wondered how his product had lost its quality.

Now, as any innovator knows, facing a quandary forces you to think beyond your previous thinking. The first thing Shorty did was to bring a stopwatch with him to work to time the rocks. This eventually confirmed that there were indeed differences in his sheets' playing speed from day to day. Although it now seems patently obvious, Shorty's in-depth investigation helped him realize for the first time that the temperature outside was impacting the ice's texture.

Later, Shorty figured out that 23°F (–5°C) was the ideal temperature inside the curling rink. At 17°F (–8°C), though, frost would start forming on the ice, which would cause stones to slow down. This simple realization is what led to Shorty's revolutionary "swing" ice. In all likelihood, this initial experience with the wisdom of stones helped Shorty formulate his professional philosophy, which states that "a curling rock is smarter than a human being." Put differently, Shorty had realized that a curling rock knows when the ice is second-rate long before a human being does.

Of course, the revolution in ice making didn't happen overnight. After his first epiphany about the outside temperature and humidity, Shorty began recording temperatures inside the curling club. Then, after competing in the 1974 Ontario playdowns and realizing that the ice wasn't ideal, Shorty stopped curling in order to study additional factors, such as air flow, scraping patterns, water types and pebbling density. Then he studied the stones themselves to figure out how rocks curl and how other factors might have an impact on a rock's swing. Little by little, Jenkins developed an encyclopedic knowledge of ice conditions and curling stones that helped him maintain near-perfect ice conditions. Ultimately, his trial-and-error scientific method taught Shorty and his disciples how to control the various vital factors that determine how a rock will glide over a curling sheet. Part art and part science, Shorty's method has now been the industry standard for over three decades. His goal has always been to make any shot playable, so that ice conditions don't affect a curler's strategy. Like a good referee, he has never wanted his work to interfere with the game.

Now a swinging septuagenarian, Clarence Shorty Jenkins has retired from the bigger curling competitions, thereby depriving the mainstream from seeing one of curling's most charismatic icons. Even sadder is that Shorty was recently diagnosed with Alzheimer's disease. And although many of his secrets have been passed on to friends and colleagues such as Dave Merklinger and Hans Wuthrich, who together will be in charge of the ice at the 2010 Olympics in Vancouver, it is perhaps fitting that Shorty may have kept a few tricks of the trade to himself. That way, his disciples will be forced to discover their own tricks, rather than getting everything on a silver platter.

Paul Gowsell

Although he is still going strong, Paul Gowsell is curling's version of Richie Valens. A shooting star who arrived on the scene full of flash and dash, Gowsell turned the curling world upside down. Then, like a hurricane passing through town, he was gone, leaving plenty of debris in his wake. This, at any rate, is one of the prevalent myths about Gowsell. And it might just be true. Let's take a look at his career.

Gowsell's reign as the bad boy of curling began in 1976, when he led his team of Alberta juniors to the first of two World Junior Championships. That year, he entered the spotlight not because he won, but because he was a wild dude from Calgary who loved to tear things up. In effect, Gowsell was a hippie with an anti-establishment streak. He drove a VW van, had a big red beard, long and wiry red hair and he wore those loud plaid pants that were all the rage in the disco era of the late '70s. And if his attire was flamboyant, it was nothing compared to his personality.

Gowsell liked to party, and when I say party, I mean haaarrrd!

There are of course countless stories of Gowsell's drinking and carousing, but let's resign ourselves to only a few. First, after winning the Canadian junior men's championship in 1976, the party started at a high school in Edmonton, where kids were dancing the night away. Gowsell got up on stage, grabbed the mic and invited everyone back to his hotel room for a drink. Now, if you're familiar with Andy Kaufman (who Jim Carrey played in *The Man on the Moon*), then you may know that after *his* big night playing Carnegie Hall in New York, he had the temerity to invite his entire audience out for milk and cookies. Gowsell's style was a little harder, the drink being liquor, but both men were clearly prone to going overboard.

Another notorious Gowsell moment occurred at a bonspiel in Saskatoon when he got hungry mid-match and decided to order a pizza. While the game was being played, a pizza delivery boy sauntered through the arena and handed the pizza to Gowsell. With the audience in shock, some of them laughing and some of them shaking their heads in disbelief, Gowsell ate his pizza. Gowsell wasn't greedy, though, and to his credit he did offer the pizza to his opponents.

Although the hot-headed Saskatchewan skip Larry McGrath turned down the offer, the pizza may have played a role in the outcome of the match. According to legend, McGrath stepped into the hack in the final end needing a draw to win the game, but his shot came up short. Surprised that he had missed, McGrath took a look at his rock and found an olive stuck to the bottom.

With such stellar material, it is tempting to cast Gowsell as the bad boy of curling. As BC's Brent Pierce once said, "He was the McEnroe of curling." But the McEnroe comparison is appropriate on more than one level, because Gowsell was a stud of a curler in addition to being something of a clown. Despite a single Brier appearance in 1980, Gowsell won more money than seemed possible at the time. In 1978, his team won $70,000; the next year, they won another 70 grand; and in 1980, on top of going to the Brier, his team pocketed 40 grand. He also, despite the partying, practiced feverishly to ensure he was always in game shape, and his superlative shot-making never left a doubt in anyone's mind as to the calibre of his game. In a team game, however, Gowsell was probably too pronounced as an individual to sustain his greatness.

Indeed, Paul Gowsell simply moved on to other things after his Brier appearance, though he has always remained an active curler. The word on the street is that he still shows up at various events in Calgary, where he works and lives and curls. And apparently, he is pretty much the same wild character curling fans fondly remember.

Factspiel

Paul Gowsell was the first Canadian to use a push broom instead of the traditional corn broom.

Ed Werenich (b. 1947)

Known as "The Wrench" because he could ratchet up the pressure on *and* off the ice, Eddie Werenich played an aggressive and entertaining style. Never afraid to put rocks in play to see which skip was a better clutch shot-maker, Werenich was a fierce competitor who loved to battle. Although born in the small prairie town of Benito along the Saskatchewan/Manitoba border, The Wrench moved to Toronto as a teenager and has always been identified as an Ontario curler and a Toronto firefighter.

In 1972, Werenich's curling career started when he shot second for Paul Savage. Throughout the '70s, their team was pretty hit-and-miss, and in 1981, Werenich decided to skip his own team. But it wasn't until the two reunited with Werenich as skip that they found the right chemistry. Come to think of it, sheer curling talent may have had more to do with their winning the Brier in 1983 than chemistry. In addition to Werenich and Savage, Team Ontario also boasted the supremely gifted front end of Neil Harrison and John Kawaja.

Collectively, it was an exciting team to watch. With Werenich calling the shots, there were usually a lot of stones in play. Add to that John Kawaja's youth, power and charisma, and curling almost seemed like a hip sport for a while.

The Wrench also made one of his more famous on-ice calls that year by yelling at his sweepers to "sweep the piss out of it." For the next 10 years, Werenich remained a top-flight curler, while also establishing himself as a royal pain in the butt for the CCA, whose hog-line officials he labelled a bunch of "freeloading blind mice." He also mooned a CCA official, and he has been a loud and outspoken critic of the CCA's ability to manage not only the game but their own finances.

Much of the tension between The Wrench and the CCA began in 1987 when, during the Canadian Olympic trials to determine who would represent Canada in the 1988 Olympics in Calgary, a CCA official insisted that if Werenich won the trials, he would have to shed a few pounds before representing Canada. Now, obviously The Wrench was none too pleased about the request. Especially given the fact that curlers have never been beacons of health and wellness.

But from the CCA's perspective, the stakes were high. Curling may only have been a demonstration sport that year, but it was the first time since 1924 that the sport had a place in the Olympics. So everyone in the curling world realized that with a good showing, it might gain full-medal status for the following Winter Olympics. What the CCA failed to realize is that people don't watch curling because its stars are superb athletes. Rather, we watch because it is a thinking person's sport in which strategy is more important than physique. Not only that, but characters like The Wrench also make for compelling curling, and the CCA's short-sighted request was an insult to the spirit of the sport, regardless that curling did indeed find its place in the Olympics as a medal sport.

Guy Hemmings (b. 1962)

Guy Hemmings is one of those rare individuals who bridges divisions and finds common ground. Affectionately dubbed The Clown Prince of Curling, he has been a promoter, an ambassador, a teacher, a trainer and a TV analyst. As a curling personality, perhaps his most valuable trait is his ability to cross generational lines by appealing to the game's stodgy Victorian roots, while also touching a chord with younger fans who find it easy to relate to his charisma.

Fundamentally, Hemmings is a happy-go-lucky guy who curled well and had fun doing it. Never afraid to crack a joke, tell a witty story or play the prankster, Hemmings became the most popular curler Québec has produced. Obviously, he is well liked in his native Québec, but his Brier performances in 1998 (in Winnipeg) and 1999 (in Edmonton) established him as a national hero, loved across the board.

Speaking of boards, one of Hemmings' signature moments occurred in 1998 when he changed the manual scoreboard during a blackout at the Winnipeg Arena. Perhaps recalling the notorious 1971 Brier in Québec City, in which the equally charismatic Matt Baldwin arranged his team's eight rocks together in the house during a blackout, Hemmings won the approval of Western fans with this light-hearted gesture.

Then, the following year in Edmonton, Hemmings drew roars of approval when he mocked his own diminutive stature by crouching down to peer through the legs of Saskatchewan skip Gerald Shymko, known in the curling ranks as the "Jolly Green Giant." In Ottawa in 2001, Hemmings put a hockey helmet on after an advertising sign fell off one of the Civic Centre's walls. And finally, in the 2003 Halifax Brier, he was seen reading a copy of Bob Weeks' book *Curling for Dummies*. In short, Hemmings has many tricks up his sleeve. And although he never won a Brier, he has made an indelible mark on curling.

Since retiring from the game in 2003, Hemmings has remained active in the sport that seems to give him so much fun. Fought over by the CCA and the World Curling Tour, Hemmings chose the CCA, with whom he has toured across Canada promoting the game. Unfortunately, in typical curling fashion, the tour's name relies on a bad pun: it is the Rockin' the House Tour. What is it with curling and bad puns? And when will the insanity end?

Colleen Jones (b. 1959)

Colleen Jones has seen the ups and downs of the women's curling circuit. A six-time Canadian champion and two-time world champion, she is an intense competitor who has aged like fine wine. The only trouble with this metaphor is that there is nothing particularly sophisticated about Jones. There are flaws to her game, and she has been an underdog most of her career. And yet she has emerged as the most successful female skip in Canadian curling history. Indeed, Jones is a prime example of how, in curling, age and experience usually trump youthful exuberance.

In 1982, with a broadcasting degree from Dalhousie University in her back pocket, Jones, at 23, led her Nova Scotia team to the Canadian women's championship. Despite this precocious success, Jones didn't immediately turn into Canada's sweetheart, a fact that had much to do with the primacy of family and career throughout the '80s. Hired by CBC as a reporter in 1986, Jones covered various sporting events, and today she works for CBC *Newsworld* as their weather and sports reporter. During this period, Jones also had two children, which quite naturally limited the number of events she could enter.

But by the time the '90s were winding down, Jones was hitting her stride. Older and less self-critical, she started winning bonspiels again. Amazingly, 1999 saw her win a second Canadian women's championship, her first in 17 years. Then she got on a roll. Although her team failed to win the 2000 Scott Tournament of Hearts, they rebounded in 2001, and then again in 2002 and in 2003, and one last time in 2004.

In what must be considered one of professional sports' most remarkable comebacks, Jones went from being viewed as a perennial underdog to being the perennial favourite. And although she has faded slightly since her last national and world championship in 2004, she recently set her mind on representing Canada at the 2010 Winter Olympics in Vancouver. The new team, with members from across Canada, isn't eligible to play in provincial and national championships. Their focus, however, will be on cashspiels and building towards the Olympic trials. Of course, the team that emerges from the Olympic trials will then represent Canada in the 2010 Games, and if that happens, it will prove to be a crowning achievement for Jones.

There is, however, another angle to the Jones story, and it has to do with her reception and reputation within the curling rank and file. As Dean Gemmell pointed out when she was a guest on *The Curling Show*, Jones has been a polarizing figure in curling circles. Gemmell went on to wonder why Jones is "popular among many, but resented by others." It was a good question, and one that Jones predictably had difficulty dealing with.

First of all, let's take a look at her popularity. It goes without saying that success in any sport breeds fan support. After all, despite the cult of the underdog, most people appreciate watching supreme talent and skilful determination at work. But when you watch Jones at work, she doesn't necessarily ooze talent. She is more of a hard-nosed grinder who wills herself and her team to victory. And it is perhaps this latter quality that people cling to as a reason to resent her. She wins, but it is rarely convincing, or graceful. And it is possible that whereas persevering grinders in hockey are lauded for their hard work, such qualities are not seen as stimulating in women's curling.

Furthermore, it is possible that her lukewarm treatment speaks of a rift between the old guard of curling and its modern incarnation as a diverse sport that welcomes not only men but women, the disabled, the blind. In short, as curling struggles to re-brand itself as a modern and sexier game, perhaps Colleen Jones elucidates many elements of that struggle.

Born and bred in Halifax, Jones has come to personify the liberated modern woman. This doesn't mean that she's a raging feminist. What it means is that Jones has maintained an admirable balance between her curling passion, her broadcasting career and her nuclear family. In other words, she is like most curlers.

On the other hand, in more traditional terms—and curling is, let us remind ourselves, rooted in traditional and patriarchal values—Jones plays both male and female roles. Now, this is not to put her femininity into question. When men watch her squeak out victories with her relatively defensive game plan, they may appreciate her rigour, but let's just say it's not like watching Maria Sharapova gliding lithely around a tennis court while pounding the snot out of an overwhelmed opponent. In the latter case, men are seduced by the thrilling beauty of a dominant woman. When Jones throws stones, on the other hand, it is like watching a third-line hockey player grind his way into a starring role on the first line. Put simply, Jones' greatness is understated, which likely suits her just fine.

Sandra Schmirler (1963–2000)

Despite her premature passing at the age of 36, "Schmirler the Curler" had carved a reputation for herself as one of the planet's greatest curlers of all-time. And if you've seen her play, you know why. In a nutshell, she was a brilliant tactician, a dominant shooter and a commanding leader. As the ever-candid Colleen Jones once said about playing against Schmirler, "When you played her, you were in awe. You knew she was better. You knew she was going to beat you. It was like playing against Gretzky."

A three-time Canadian and World champion (1993, 1994 and 1997), Team Schmirler also won the first women's Olympic gold in the Nagano

Olympics of 1998. More than anything else, this triumph thrust Schmirler into not just the national spotlight, but the international spotlight. Naturally, the inclusion of curling as a full-medal Olympic sport in 1998 has propelled the sport onto the global stage. And in many ways, Sandra Schmirler was curling's first global ambassador. Her curling greatness, along with a keen wit and classically Canadian ironic sense of humour, helped market the women's game in ways it wouldn't have been able to earlier in the sport's history. Sadly and ironically, her struggle with cancer and subsequent death also played a role in bringing curling into the spotlight.

Born in the small prairie town of Biggar, Saskatchewan, Schmirler, like most female curlers, balanced work with family life. Curling sometimes got in the way, as it did when she curled while pregnant at the 1997 Scott Tournament of Hearts. But despite earning the nickname "Schmirler the Hurler" from one broadcaster after she took a time-out to throw up, she managed to win the tournament and then had her first of two daughters later that year.

It was after her second daughter's birth, in 1999, that Schmirler's life took an unexpected turn for the worse. Sparing the gritty details of battling cancer, suffice it to say that it was a war she couldn't win. Given her stature in Canada, however, people wanted to know how she was doing, and when she spoke about her grave condition, Schmirler provided her fans with a heartwarming perspective. In 2000, while working as a colour commentator for CBC during a junior curling championship in Moncton, she held a press conference to address her condition. After revealing the hardship she was going through, Schmirler concluded with a few wishes she had clung to during her struggle.

"There were three goals I had coming out of this thing, and the first one was to look after my family. And the second one...because I curl so much, I've never taken a hot vacation, so I'm going to put my feet in the sand in a warm place. And the last one was to actually be here today."

Not long after this public address, Schmirler died at the age of 36. Such was the impact of what Jean Chrétien called "her bright, engaging personality and her incredible zest for life," that her funeral was broadcast nationally. On March 5, 2000, two days after her passing, hundreds of thousands of Canadians tuned in to TSN and CBC to mourn the death of a Canadian icon.

Russ Howard (b. 1956)

Russ Howard is one of the sharpest tools in the shed. Technically, he has always been a flawless curler. He has a great mind for the game, and then there is his patented roar—likely the loudest the game has ever heard.

Along with his more subdued brother Glenn, the Howard brothers have been two of the game's greatest curlers since the late 80s when they came on the scene. Although they have recently split up now that Russ is living and curling out of New Brunswick, some of their best years came with Russ skipping Team Ontario and Glenn shooting third, as they won the national and world championships in 1987 and again in 1993.

Despite all of his success, it is perhaps as an innovator and as a TV analyst that Russ Howard will leave his most distinctive mark on the game. First, as an innovator, Howard initiated the Moncton Rule—so-called because it was first used in the Moncton 100 bonspiel in 1990. The rule, which is now more commonly referred to as the Free Guard Zone, stipulates that rocks positioned between the hog line and the tee line cannot be removed by the opposition until the first four rocks have been played. More simply, it allows more rocks to remain in play, in part because the rocks behind these guards are temporarily protected.

Without question, the advent of this rule has made curling a far more entertaining sport than it once was, when defensive strategies reigned.

Secondly, as a colour commentator, Howard is an extremely skilled communicator, which helps him convey the intricacies and strategies of the game in vivid ways. Although he has just started in this capacity, he has the ability to do for curling what John McEnroe did for tennis.

Factspiel

In the 2006 Winter Olympics in Torino, Russ Howard joined forces with Newfoundland's Brad Gushue to win gold for Canada. At 50 years old, Howard became the oldest athlete to win a gold medal at the Olympics.

Randy Ferbey vs. Kevin Martin

For years, it has been virtually impossible to talk about Randy Ferbey without talking about Kevin Martin, and vice versa. Not only are both men from Edmonton, but they also happen to be pretty firmly established as the two best curlers in the world today. Or, at the very least, they have the two best rinks. But they also have a history that is as messy as Paul Gowsell's coif.

For starters, the two men were on different sides of the fence when curling had its cold war. In 2001–02, when the World Curling Tour strong-armed the Canadian Curling Association by forcing players to choose between the two organizations, Martin led the splinter group, while Ferbey and his cohorts refused to be pressured into taking drastic action. Now, while their respective positions during those rocky times for the curling fraternity may shed some light on their respective characters, the juicier bits have to do with their on-ice rivalry and the little jabs at each other that have provided the media with some sweet fodder for the better part of a decade.

For his part, Randy Ferbey often seems stuck between bemusement and anger when he talks about Kevin Martin. Ferbey, who kept playing in the Brier while the Grand Slammers played exclusively for money, is miffed by the smugness and underhanded tactics Martin has employed over the years. In the 2007 book *The Ferbey Four* by Terry Jones, Ferbey's team express their feelings towards Martin through the candid language of direct quotes. After reading the chapter "More Than a Rivalry," it is clearly expressed in a number of ways that while Martin's game is greatly respected, his character is, to be blunt, detested. In short, the problem seems to lie in Martin's megalomania. As Ferbey's vice-skip Dave Nedohin once put it, "[Martin] thinks he's God. He always will."

Of course, Ferbey played briefly for Martin in the early '90s, but after coming up short in a few bonspiels, Martin more or less cut Ferbey. Later on, Martin also had the chance to axe Ferbey's current third, Marcel Rocque. So there is some degree of internal turmoil between the two highly competitive men and their rinks.

If one thing is clear, however, it is that their personalities go together like water and oil. Ferbey is a laid-back guy with a genuine personality. He is imminently quotable, and he seems like a stellar guy to have a beer with. Martin, on the other hand, just flat-out wins games. But he never gives you the impression that he's having a blast doing it. Fair enough. Curling is now a business, after all, with good money at stake if you can win it. And Martin certainly can. What irks Ferbey's team, though, is Martin's inability or outright refusal to give credit when credit is due. Again, in *The Ferbey Four*, Marcel Rocque recounts the aftermath of an M&M Skins Game in which Team Ferbey beat Team Martin:

"It was a game when the ice got bad. We left him a shot on the outside he had no chance to make. Kevin was standing there being interviewed and, as always, he wasn't giving us any credit for a victory. Randy Ferbey was walking off the ice and we both made a couple of comments about that. And somehow Randy and I started on about who despised Kevin most and who was first. Looking back, it was hilarious. As I remember it, it wasn't so hilarious at the time."

As a fan, though, whoever you happen to cheer for is not as crucial as the fact that their personality clash has provided some much-needed drama in the world of curling. After all, what is a sport without enemies who despise each other?

The Curling Show

Dean Gemmell is a unique figure in the world of curling. With an advertising background as a copywriter for such firms as Young & Rubicam, Doner and Ogilvy & Mather, Gemmell started *The Curling Show* of his own accord in 2005. Since then, he has recorded podcasts from, of all places, Short Hills, New Jersey.

While you may not think of the Jersey shores as a curling mecca—and it certainly isn't—*The Curling Show* is quite simply the most informative curling talk show the curling world has seen. As stated on the show's website, *The Curling Show* is a "podcast that brings you interviews with the sport's top athletes and the people who shape the game." Oh yeah, and he's a fan of the ironic metal band Black Pudding, whose line "I wanna rock! If you know what I mean..." is the podcast's opening line. The band also has a killer song called "Rockaholic."

The host is young, deadpan and knowledgeable about curling and the business and marketing of the game. And unlike television interviews that tend to elicit pat and clichéd responses, Gemmell gets to the meat of important issues that face the world of curling.

Chapter Seven

The Greatest Moments in Curling History

Curling is steeped in both tradition and stories. But it is also about making clutch shots and thrilling finishes that go down to the wire. In the final end, of course, the pressure to deliver a precise shot is magnified. For those who rise to the occasion and deliver a clutch shot, they create curling glory for themselves. And for those who blow it with the game hanging in the balance, they are ruthlessly remembered as chokers. But therein lies the beauty of sports. And curling is no different.

Orest Meleschuk vs. Bob LaBonte

1972 Air Canada Silver Broom Final
Garmisch-Partenkirchen, Bavaria, Germany
Final score: Canada 10, USA 9

In the 1972 Air Canada Silver Broom, a now-defunct tournament that determined the world champion, Canada was pitted against the U.S. in the final. The Canadian team, led by legendary skip Orest Meleschuk, was the heavy favourite, having already disposed of their Scottish rivals in the semi-final.

But in the 10th and final end, Bob LaBonte and his U.S. team were ahead by 9–7, and even though Meleschuk had the hammer, things looked grim for the Canadian squad. With his last stone in hand, Meleschuk faced a difficult shot just to score two and force an extra end.

Needing a hit-and-stick to leave two shot rocks, Meleschuk stepped into the hack with a cigarette dangling from the corner of his mouth. With the clunky delivery of an old-time curler, his rock slid the length of the ice and knocked the American stone out of play.

Unfortunately, his aim was slightly off, and instead of getting a hit-and-stick, he got a hit-and-roll. By the time his stone came to rest at the edge of the 8-foot, it appeared that the U.S. stone beside it was closer to the button. Although a measurement was likely in order, it appeared that the Americans had won. Until something truly bizarre happened.

After taking a quick look at the position of the stones, U.S. third Frank Aasand raised his broom in celebration. Then LaBonte entered the picture.

Coming from behind the house to join Aasand in celebration, LaBonte jumped up, landed on his heels and slipped as if on a banana peel. With his legs flying around awkwardly, he grazed or "burned" the Canadian stone, thereby moving it a few inches closer to the button. The burn, however, was enough to force an extra end. Unfortunately for the U.S., neither Aasand nor LaBonte noticed the burn, so they simply measured the rocks based on the new alignment. The Canadian stone was now closer.

In the extra end, the Canadians had momentum on their side, and it carried them to a world championship victory. It was, however, one of the oddest finishes in curling history, and it made Bob LaBonte a household name.

Factspiel

After losing the world championship final, Bob LaBonte added a little fuel to the fire by placing a curse on Canada and its future curlers; he swore that Canada would never again win a World Championship. For the next seven years, the curse gained validity, as Canada went through the longest international drought it had ever seen. Mercifully, Rick Folk and his team from Saskatchewan ended the drought in 1980, thereby breaking "the curse of LaBonte."

Kerry Burtnyk vs. Al Hackner

1981 Brier Final
Halifax, Nova Scotia
Final score: Manitoba 5, Northern Ontario 4

Throughout his career, Al Hackner was known as "The Iceman" because he was so cool under pressure. But in the 1981 Brier final, it was Burtnyk who rose to the occasion. Down 4–2 going into the final end, the 22-year-old Burtnyk had last rock advantage, with victory looking out of reach. Somehow, Burtnyk's aggressive game and youthful moxie allowed him to keep everything in check, and his team scored three in the final end, giving his team the upset and making him the youngest skip to win the Brier.

Ed Werenich vs. Bernie Sparkes

1983 Brier Semi-final
Sudbury, Ontario
Final score: Ontario 6, British Columbia 3

In the sixth end of the 1983 Brier semi-final, the game turned on its head. In typical Werenich fashion, there were loads of stones in play, but in this instance, most of them belonged to BC's Bernie Sparkes. So The Wrench sized things up and chose the gutsiest option he had: a triple takeout. He leaned back, let 'er rip and made a miraculous shot that swung the end and the game decidedly in his favour. After dispatching Sparkes, Werenich went on to beat Alberta for the national title, before rolling through the competition at that year's World Championships.

Al Hackner vs. Pat Ryan
1985 Brier Final
Moncton, New Brunswick
Final score: Northern Ontario 6, Alberta 5

In curling circles, it is simply known as The Shot. Like Joe Carter's walk-off home run to win the World Series, or Paul Henderson's game-winning goal against the Soviets in 1972, Al Hackner's shot in the 1985 Brier final is curling's signature moment. The reason it stands out above all other shots is two-fold. First, it was Hackner's last chance to snatch victory from the jaws of defeat. And second, it was a circus shot so improbable that Siegfried & Roy would have scoffed at his odds.

The final took place on March 10, 1985, at the Moncton Coliseum, and Pat Ryan's Alberta team was the heavy favourite. The Ryan Express was known for its heavy-hitting defensive style. Like the New Jersey Devils of the 1990s, Ryan's teams won by getting a lead and then sitting on it, taking no chances. It was a disciplined system, and it worked beautifully. Remember, these were the days before Russ Howard invented the Free Guard Zone, which he designed to usher aggressive and offensive strategies back into the game. But in Pat Ryan's era, he was the master of shutting the game down once he got ahead. So with his team (which had gone 11–0 in the tournament leading up to the final) up 5–3 going into the 10th and final end, nobody gave Hackner a chance in hell. But being the accomplished drinker he was, Hackner had ice in his veins.

Somehow, after a few shots, Ryan let Hackner get two guards in play, and it was Hackner's turn to make magic. With his first stone, Hackner played a textbook split that left him lying one with another stone on the 12-foot.

Then Ryan stepped up to the plate. With three stones in the rings (Hackner had an open one on the 4-foot and another on the 12-foot, while Ryan had one in between on the 8-foot), Ryan played a perfect hit-and-roll off Hackner's stone in the 4-foot. With it, Ryan was now lying two, and both stones were well covered. Hackner seemed finished.

As Hackner stepped into the hack, the crowd of 5176 fell silent. It was clear that The Iceman's only shot was a razor-thin double takeout. To make it, he needed to slide past his own guard by the thinnest of margins in order to take out the first Ryan stone. Then his shooter needed to stretch across the house to take out the second Ryan stone. Only then would he lie two and send the game to an extra end. After the match, Hackner recounted his mindset: "I could see about an inch of the rock and I had to hit half an inch. I remember sitting in the hack thinking I'd made two or three razzle-dazzle shots before in club games and if I had one more razzle-dazzle in me let it be now."

Sure enough, he let the stone go and so did the sweepers. As the stone inched past the guard by the thinnest of margins, it was clear that the stars had aligned. Hackner nailed the shot, and Moncton erupted. With more momentum on his side than a jackknifed 18-wheeler, Hackner won the game in an extra end. It took a measurement, and Hackner's rock was a measly inch or so closer to the button, but after making The Shot, there was never really any doubt.

Russ Howard vs. Bernie Sparkes
1987 Brier Final
Edmonton, Alberta
Final score: Ontario 11, British Columbia 7

Tied at four after the seventh end, this nail-biter suddenly turned into a barn-burner. In the eighth, Howard took two with the hammer and went up

6–4. In the ninth, though, Sparkes answered with three of his own to take the lead heading into the final end. It all came down to Howard's last rock. Sparkes was lying one, but Howard had a bead on it. He later called it "the toughest shot I've had to throw in my life." But he made the clutch shot and scored a whopping five.

Sandra Schmirler vs. Shannon Kleibrink

1997 Canadian Olympic Trials
Brandon, Manitoba
Final score: Saskatchewan 9, Alberta 6

Having finished first in the Olympic Trials' round-robin, Schmirler advanced directly to the final, while Kleibrink disposed of BC's Kelley Law in the lone semi-final. The final was a see-saw affair, and in the seventh end, Schmirler was down 4–3, and Kleibrink had a stone on the button with a few well-positioned guards out front. Schmirler was in trouble, and her only option was to play off one of her own stones on the outskirts of the house. Her shot was thrown perfectly as she hit-and-rolled right into the button, picking out Kleibrink's stone to score three and take a 6–4 lead. From there, she cruised to victory and went on to beat Denmark in the Olympic final to claim gold in Nagano.

Guy Hemmings vs. Gerald Shymko

1999 Brier Semi-final
Edmonton, Alberta
Final score: Québec 6, Saskatchewan 5

In the 1999 Brier semi-final, Hemmings and Shymko went to extra ends knotted at five. Of course, it came down to the final stone, and Hemmings had the hammer. Shymko, however, was sitting pretty with a well-guarded rock that was nibbling at the button. With no takeout option, Hemmings had to show perfect touch by drawing to the absolute centre of the button. Excellent sweeping also played a role, but Hemmings threw the perfect draw weight to send Shymko packing.

Hammy McMillan vs. Jeff Stoughton

1999 World Championship Final
Saint John, New Brunswick
Final score: Scotland 6, Canada 5

Despite inventing curling and golf, the Scottish have by-and-large been mediocre at both sports. In the world championships of curling, Scotland has prevailed a measly four times—in 1967, 1991, 1999 and 2006. One of the Scottish curling legends, though, is a rather rowdy character by the name of Hammy McMillan. With five European championships to his credit, he saved his best for Canada's Jeff Stoughton in the world championship final in Saint John, New Brunswick.

McMillan won an exciting game by the score of 6–5, and although his ridiculous round-the-house triple takeout didn't seal the victory, it was a truly mesmerizing shot. First of all, the stone was fired down the curling sheet like a cannonball. The first Canadian stone it disposed of was on the 12-foot. The Scottish stone then continued to the back of the 12-foot, taking out a second Canadian rock. Finally, thanks to a remarkably calculated angle, the Scottish stone crossed the rings and removed Canada's final rock. With that shot, McMillan had killed three birds with one stone.

Jennifer Jones vs. Jenn Hanna

2005 Scott Tournament of Hearts Final
St. John's, Newfoundland
Final score: Manitoba 8, Ontario 6

In 2005, before Jennifer Jones had solidified her reputation as the dominant skip in women's curling, she was playing in her second Scott Tournament of Hearts and seeking her first national title. And did she ever earn it.

Down 6–4 going into the 10th end, it came down to the wire. There were plenty of stones in play, but Ontario had a well-guarded rock sitting plum on the button. The only way in was to think outside the box. Using a stone that wasn't even in the house, Jones ricocheted her rock in off the outlying stone. Amazingly, she succeeded in making the in-off and knocked the Ontario stone off the button and out of the house, leaving four of her own stones.

Because of the nature of the shot and the insane degree of difficulty involved in making it, Jones' shot quickly became known as "The Shot," thereby comparing its greatness with The Shot back in 1985, when Al Hackner won the Brier with a razor-thin double takeout.

Chapter Eight

Curling Lingo

12-foot circle: The outer circle of the house, which measures 12 feet (3.65 metres) in diameter and is normally painted red or blue.

8-foot circle: The inner circle of the house measuring 8 feet (2.4 metres) in diameter. It is usually the same colour as the ice.

A curling house consists of three rings. The outer red ring is the 12-foot; the middle white ring is the 8-foot; and the inner yellow circle is the 4-foot. At the centre of the house is the button, where this stone is lying dead centre.

4-foot circle: The final circle of the house before the button, measuring 4 feet (1.2 metres) in diameter.

Alternate: (See *Spare.*)

Back line: This is the line that runs across the ice at the back of the house. Any stone that travels over this line is automatically removed from the field of play.

Back ring: The technical term for the portion of the 8-foot and 12-foot rings that are behind the tee line.

Back ring weight: This is when the precision curler throws a rock hard enough that it stops in the back of the house.

Biter: A stone that is barely touching the 12-foot outer ring.

Blank end: When neither team scores a point in the end. (See *End.*)

Bonspiel: An organized curling tournament or competition. The bonspiel is the life blood of the curling world. The more popular bonspiels attract people from around the world.

Brier: The ultimate curling tournament. It was started in 1927 by the Macdonald Tobacco Company to decide which province in Canada would be the national champions. Every year the event takes place in a different Canadian city, and the winning team earns the right to represent Canada on the international stage.

Broom: Although no longer commonly used, the broom is the implement with which players sweep the ice directly in front of the rock to make it travel farther. The traditional curling broom is made up of long fibres wrapped tightly together but still allowing flexibility. When used properly, the broom rapidly smacks the ice in front of the rock clearing out the rough pebbles.

Brush: The brush performs the exact same function as the broom, to make the rock travel farther and curl less. The brush has shorter bristles and requires less movement than the traditional broom. The brush is the standard tool for most curlers, but some still stubbornly stick to the old broom.

Burned stone or rock: A moving stone touched by a member of either team or with any part of their equipment. When this occurs the burned stone is removed from play.

Bury a stone: When a player curls in a stone behind a guard.

Button: The circle at the centre of the house; sometimes called the one-foot circle.

C

Cashspiels: Similar to bonspiels, except that curlers play for a cash prize.

Closing a port: When a shooter blocks an opponent between two rocks.

Coming home: Playing out the last end.

Corner guard: A rock placed specifically in front of the 12-foot ring and slightly to the side to help protect a rock in the corner of the house, usually behind the corner guard.

Cram-pits: Before the invention of hacks, curlers attached a cram-pit on the soles of their shoes in order to give them the grip they needed. Cram-pits were basically spikes or cleats that dug into the ice to provide a gripping surface.

D

Dead handle: A stone that loses its rotation or is not given any rotation on delivery. (See *No handle*.)

Delivery: The process of throwing the stone,

which players do by sliding out of the hack. Before they reach the first hog line, they must release the stone.

Doubles: If you can manage to string together a few doubles in a match then you certainly are a good curler. A double is a take-out shot that removes two opposing stones from the house.

Draw: Along with the takeout, the draw is one of two basic curling shots. If you play a draw, you do not intend to hit any other stone. Instead, you are attempting to draw the rock to a precise place. As a basic shot, there are several variations of the draw, including the guard, the raise and the freeze.

Draw the lid / Draw the pin: When a player draws the lid, or pin, they have made a shot that comes to a stop directly on the button.

Draw weight: The weight needed to draw your stone to a precise point in the house.

E

Eight-ender: An end where all eight stones score a point. A rare occurrence.

End: Similar to an inning in baseball. When both teams have used their eight stones, the end is over. There are usually 10 ends in a game, with the possibility of an 11th end—known as an extra end—if the game is tied after 10 ends.

F

Free guard zone: The area on the ice between the hog line and the tee line, excluding the house.

Free guard zone rule: This regulation states that you cannot take out your opponent's stone that is lying in the free guard zone until the first four stones (two by each team) have been played in that end.

Freeze: A stone that is delivered with perfect weight and comes to rest directly against another.

Frosty ice: When the sheet of ice has accumulated a layer of frost because of high humidity levels. Having frosty ice can severely affect the way a rock curls.

G

Give ice: When a player holds a brush for the skip to aim at, helping to indicate the amount of ice needed to draw to the intended target.

Gripper: In curling there are two separate

and distinct shoes. One is known as the slider (see *Slider*) and the other is called the gripper. Although there are many types of grippers, the most common has a simple rubber sole with tiny bumps to help grip the ice. The gripper is used to push the player out of the hack or to propel the player down the ice when sweeping.

Guard: A stone that comes to rest in front of another as protection. Playing the proper guard is essential to any competitive curling match.

H

Hack: The two footholds that the curler pushes out of to deliver the rock down the ice. Similar to the starting blocks used in track and field, the hack is a tochold that is used to propel the curler forward. There are two hacks placed at each end of the ice, though players only use one to throw a stone. One hack is for left-handed players, and the other is for right-handed players.

Hammer: Having the hammer means having the last rock advantage in an end.

Handle: The top part of the rock that the curler grips to deliver it down the ice. The handle is an important part of the process, because the amount of spin put on the handle affects how the rock curls down the ice.

Heavy hit: When a rock is forcefully thrown down the ice and knocks the opponent's rock out of play.

Heavy ice: Ice that has an excess amount of water, frost or pebbles, requiring more weight to deliver a stone into the house.

Hit: When a shot removes an opponent's stationary stone from play.

Hit and stick / Hit and lie / Hit and stay: When a player strikes an opponent's stone dead on so that it is knocked out of the house while the player's stone sticks, without rolling elsewhere.

Hit and roll: When a player strikes an opponent's stone and knocks it out of the house while the player's stone rolls to a new position, usually within the house where it is a threat to score.

Hit the broom: A term used to describe a shot that has accurately hit the aiming point. Before taking a shot, a teammate will place the broom at one end of the ice to indicate where the curler should aim.

Hog: The name given to a stone that fails to reach the far hog line and therefore is removed from play. (See *Hogged rock.*)

Hog line: There are two hog lines on a curling sheet. The near hog line is the one closest to the hack, and when a curler delivers a stone, he or she must release the stone before reaching the hog line. At the other end of the ice, there is a second hog line known as the far hog line. Every stone must cross this far hog line to enter the field of play. If the delivery is too short, the stone is removed from play.

Hogged rock: Another name for a stone that fails to reach the far hog line.

Hogger: (See *Hogged rock*.)

House: The house is the 12-foot wide set of concentric rings at the far end of a curling sheet. The centre of the house is marked by two lines (the tee lines) that divide the house into quarters. At the junction of these two lines is the button, or the absolute centre of the house. To score a point in curling, your stone has to be the closest stone to the button when an end comes to an end.

Hurry! Hard!: Possibly the two most famous words in curling. This is what the skips or the thirds scream at the top of their lungs to get their teammates to begin sweeping in front of the rock. The more they scream, the more their teammates have to sweep. (I'm surprised that some throat lozenge manufacturer hasn't hired a pro curler to advertise their products.)

I

Ice: No, this is not exactly the literal term for the ice underneath their feet (although it could also be just that). "Ice" in curling also refers to the distance between a rock and its desired destination.

Ice technician: The title of the person whose job it is to take care of the curling ice. It is this person's job to take care of the condition of the ice, watching for frost or water build up, and pebbling (see *Pebbles*) the ice.

In-turn: A stone that rotates in a clockwise direction for the right-handed curler.

J

Jitney (pronounced "jit-nee"): In the real world, "jitney" is defined in three separate ways.

1. A small motor vehicle, such as a car or a mini-van (or these days an SUV), that transports people on a route for a nominal fee.

2. Archaic term for a nickel.

3. In the business world, jitney is a situation in which one broker who has direct access to a stock exchange performs trades for a broker who does not have access. A fraudulent activity in the penny stock market involving two brokers trading a stock back and forth to rack up commissions and give the impression of trading volume.

The only thing is that none of the above definitions has anything to do with curling, but at least we all learned something. To add to your new lexicon in curling, a "jitney" is a game played without any serious competition; that is, played mainly for the purpose of a good time. Local curling clubs often organize jitney-themed nights for curlers and their families. A jitney is more of a social occasion that happens to occur around a game of curling.

K

Keen ice: A description used to identify fast ice, requiring less momentum in delivery.

L

Lead: The first person on a team to toss the stones in each end.

Loofie: Scottish word for the early types of stones. Derived from the word "loof," which meant the palm of the hand.

Lost the handle: A rock that loses its rotation while travelling down the ice. When a rock does not rotate, it loses its ability to curl.

M

Mate: A player's position on a team. Another term used to describe the third curler. It is the mate's responsibility to throw the fifth and sixth stones of each end. (See *Third* and *Vice*.)

Measure: In curling there are three specific definitions of measure.

1. It is a process to determine which of two stones is the closest to the centre of the house.

2. It determines whether a stone is actually in the house in the case of a close call.

3. It is also the name of the instrument used to perform the measurements to determine the above.

Narrow: Delivering a stone inside the intended line of delivery, normally demarcated by a teammate's broom at the other end of the ice.

Negative ice: An annoying part of curling that occurs when, because of poor ice conditions, stones turn in the opposite direction than they were originally intended.

Nice rock / Nice toss: A good shot.

Nose hit: A curling shot in which a delivered stone removes a rock from play and stops moving after contact. It is the perfect transference of weight and momentum to another target.

On the broom: A stone delivered accurately on line with the skip's broom that was placed as the aiming target.

Outside: Term for when a rock is shot wide or off target.

Out-turn: A simple curl of the wrist for the right-handed player that sends the rock down the ice spinning in a counter-clockwise direction.

Pebbles: One of the most essential parts of

curling. These are the small bumps on the rink that help the rock curl better. It is the sweeper's job to brush these pebbles to help the stone curl less and travel straight. Before the start of each game an ice technician purposefully applies these bumps to the ice.

Peel: A peel is a type of takeout that removes a stone from play *in addition to* the delivered stone. When you play a peel, your intention is to have your own stone carom out of play.

Pitting: Irregular indentations that form on the rim or running edge of the stone, which can severely affect the curl of the stone.

Playdown: A specific type of competition that leads into recognized curling championships. Playdowns begin at the club level but then the winner might move on to regional, national or international curling events. They are basically playoffs that decide who gets to move on to a bigger show. For club curlers, these are the most competitive and sought-after games in a curling season.

Port: An opening between two stones that is wide enough for another stone to pass through. It is a shot only made by the best curlers. The equivalent in hockey would be picking out a goalie's five-hole.

R

Raise: When a delivered stone bumps a stationary stone forward, but not out of play.

Rim: The outer portion of the cup on the bottom of the stone. The bottom of the stone has a concave shape so that the entire rock does not come into contact with the ice. It is only the rim of the stone, measuring 5–7 millimetres in width, that gives the rock its curl.

Rings: The rings at the business end of the ice. Also more commonly known as the house.

Rink: The curling word for team. A "rink" consists of four players: the first, second and third (or vice) shooters followed by the skip (captain). A "rink" is also the name given to the curling venue (more commonly used in hockey terminology).

Rock: Also referred to as a stone. This is the smooth granite stone, weighing on average 42 pounds (19 kilograms), that the curler launches down the ice. The handle attached to the top of the rock helps the curler control the rock's rotation.

Roll: The direction a stone takes after it is struck by another stone.

Run: A section of the ice that dips and changes the direction of a delivered stone.

Running edge: The part of the curling stone that touches the ice. It is between 5 and 7 millimetres in width. (See *Rim.*)

S

Second: The second player on the team who delivers the third and fourth stones during each end. The second follows the lead player.

Sheet: The strip of ice on which the game of curling is played. Curling clubs usually have several sheets of ice on which to play.

Short: A rock that stops short of its desired position.

Skip: The most important player on the team, the skip is the fourth shooter on the team who delivers the seventh and eighth stones of each end. The skip is responsible for directing the strategy of the game and is the player who usually gets all the glory.

Slider: Every curler wears a different type of shoe on each foot. One is called a gripper (see *Gripper*), used to give the player traction on the ice, and the other is called the slider. The slider is the sole of one shoe that allows the curler to move or slide along the ice surface.

Spare: An alternate player or a substitute in case of emergency.

Spinner: A rock thrown with too much rotation.

Split: Describes a curling shot in which a stationary stone is knocked into the house and the delivered stone rolls into the house as well.

Splitting the house: A curling strategy in which a team places two stones at opposite ends of the house so that the opposing team cannot take them both out easily.

Steal: When a team scores a point without last rock advantage.

Stone: (See *Rock.*)

T

Take the rock: The action of sweeping closest to the rock.

Takeout: One of curling's basic shots, the takeout is designed to remove an opponent's stone from play. There are several versions of the takeout, including the peel, and the hit and roll.

Tankard: The name of the trophy given to the winner of the Brier.

Tee: The hole in the centre of the house. Usually where a measure is placed to measure stones.

Tee line: There are two tee lines on a curling ice sheet: one that runs horizontally through the button, and one that runs vertically through the button from one end of the sheet to the other. This latter vertical line is more commonly called the centre line.

Third: Also known as the vice-skip or mate, the third is responsible for delivering the fifth and sixth rocks of each end.

Toss: The coin toss at the beginning of a game to decide which team gets the last rock in the first end.

V

Vice: (See *Third.*) The third curler on the team. Shoots the fifth and sixth rocks of each end.

W

Weight: The momentum applied to a rock on delivery.

Weld: The perfect freeze; when the rock comes to rest in direct contact with another rock without moving it.

Wick: To hit an opponent's rock with the lightest of touches. "His shot wicked the opponent's inside the house."

Z

Zones: Areas of interest on the curling playing surface.

Chapter Nine

Curling Time Line

(circa) 1500s: Although there is some historical dispute as to whether Scotland or Holland introduced the game of curling to early 16th-century society, Holland largely falls from the books. Scotland comes out the pioneer and leader in bringing the roaring game to the rest of the world in the following centuries.

(circa) 1500–1650: The stone used in curling during this time period was known as the Kuting-Stone, Kutty-Stane, Piltycock or Loofie. The stone did not have a handle, and players inserted their finger or thumb into a small, hollowed-out opening in the rock. Weighing between five and 25 pounds (2–11 kilograms), these stones were smaller than ones made later with handles and were thrown rather than slid along the ice, because rinks back then were much shorter.

(circa) 1540–41: The first documented game of curling takes place, between a monk named John Sclater and the Abbot's deputy, Gavin Hamilton. Although there is some variance on the exact year, and Scottish curling historian Reverend John Kerr wrote that no Scottish historians or poets made reference to the act of curling before 1600, this general opinion changed in 1976. A professor of Scottish history, John Durkan, found the papers of notary John McQuhin of Scotland, and they contained words referencing the game played by Sclater and Hamilton of throwing stones on ice.

1551: Found many years after the fact, the well-known Stirling Stone, inscribed with this date, is discovered when an old pond in Dunblane, Scotland, is drained. It is widely believed to be the oldest curling stone ever found anywhere in the world.

1565: Looking back at the history of curling, and knowing the game began sometime in the early 1500s, historians can identify two of the earliest visual records of the game from this time. Dutch painter Pieter Bruegel twice portrayed a game called "ice shooting" (a Bavarian game played with a long, stick-like handle), in *Winter Landscape with Skaters and a Birdtrap* and *Hunters in the Snow* in 1565.

(circa) late 1500s, early 1600s: A curling-like game is shown in an engraving by R. de Baudous, depicting players who look like they're sliding large discs of wood along a small body of frozen water. Other drawings from this time period also show a Dutch game called kuting, similar to curling as curlers know it today, but it was played with frozen lumps of earth.

1620: After the back-and-forth historical disputes about the origins and advent of the game, the word "curling," in the correct context, appears in a poem by Henry Adamson, marking his use of the word as the first time it actually shows up in a text. Written about a friend who had recently passed away, Adamson's poem references the game in the following manner: "His name was M. James Gall, a citizen of Perth, and a gentle-man of goodly stature, and pregnant wit, much given to pastime, as golf, archerie, curling and jovial companie."

1638: The Scots love their curling—so much so that Bishop Graham of Orkney disobeys the religious rules of the day, as did other Scottish curlers of the time, but they don't make the history books as famously as Bishop Graham. The Bishop is accused of curling on the Sabbath, an offence thought to be terrible enough to have been documented in the days when strict observance of the day of rest on Sunday was a matter, apparently, not to be taken lightly!

(circa) 1650–1800: It was time to say goodbye to the Kuting-Stone and hello to the Rough Block. Because quite a few of these stones are preserved today, historians know that the rocks had a handle, unlike their earlier counterparts, but they were bulkier and heavier. Made from stones often taken from a streambed or from a hillside, these rocks had a bent piece of iron inserted into the stone as the handle. Weighing anywhere from 20 to 115 pounds (9–52 kilograms), the stones were heavy. Fortunately, rinks were still small in the 17th and 18th centuries.

1668: The first curling club is founded in Scotland in Kinross, Loch Leven.

(circa) 1700: Curling gains popularity in Scotland and becomes a common sport to play at any skill level. There is no more reason to dispute the documentation of the word "curling" or whether or not it was played—many texts from this time period describe bonspiels and curling societies and hail curling as a great Scottish game.

1760: Sometime in the early 18th century, Scots immigrating to Canada bring the game of curling with them, finding Canadian winters to be perfect for the sport. In the Québec winter of 1760, Scottish troops from the 78th Fraser Highland Regiment melt down cannon balls to make curling irons (for the ice, not for their hair). This event marks the first time the iron curling stone is ever made or played with anywhere else but Canada. The anomaly is that the iron curling "stone" is shaped like a tea kettle; men's irons weighed 60–80 pounds (27–36 kilograms), while women's weighed 40–48 pounds (18–21 kilograms).

1771: Although curling had been written about earlier, a description of an actual match was yet to be documented, and this happens in 1771 when James Graeme, a 22-year-old divinity student, has his words on the subject published in *Weekly Magazine*.

(circa) late 1700s: Curlers today turn the stone when they make their play, but this was not always the case in the history of curling—stones were just basically thrown up and the down the ice. However, curlers in

Fenwick, Scotland, discover around the late
18th century that if the stone is thrown with
a turn (or as it was called then, a "twist") it
will often end up behind a rival player's and
therefore be hidden. Many followers of the
game do not take well to this new technique,
calling it illegal and rallying for it to be
outlawed—it was simply unacceptable! Other
followers think they can beat the curlers of
Fenwick at their own game and employ the
turn as well, and so, competition for the game
wins out and the in-turn and out-turn of
curling are born.

(circa) 1800: From the Kuting-Stone to the
Rough Block, the curling stone had gone
through various transformations since
the Stirling Stone of 1551. Around 1800,
however, the Circular Stone is crafted, only
to morph, essentially into the type of stone
curlers use today. Weighing sometimes
up to 70 pounds (31 kilograms), circular
curling stones become the more uniform and
accepted rock throughout the sport of curling,
causing the earlier variety of shapes to slowly
be put on the shelf.

1804: With the popularity of curling on the
rise and with more games being played
as professionally as was possible in the

early 19th century, rules were needed for newcomers and to settle disputes. The Duddingston Club in Scotland, established in 1795, is the first club to create of set of rules for curling—rules that end up being very similar to the ones curlers follow today.

1807: The first North American curling club is established in January by 20 merchants in Montréal who curl on the ice of the St. Lawrence River. Named the Montréal Curling Club, not only is the club the first of its kind in North America, but it also gains the distinction of being the first curling club established outside of Scotland.

(circa) 1831, 1832: The Orchard Lake Curling Club of Detroit makes its debut as the first curling club in the U.S. The club was founded by Scottish farmers, who, as history tells it, immigrated to Chicago and were shipwrecked on the shore of Lake St. Clair, where they stayed, and they began curling with "stones" fashioned out of hickory. Not long after, Boston (1839), Milwaukee (1843) and Chicago (1854) also form their own curling clubs.

1837: The first indoor rink in Canada is created by the curlers of Ste. Anne de Bellevue in the province of Québec. A curling shed is built, with water poured on the wooden floor and then allowed to freeze. Sounds rudimentary, but the indoor curling rinks of today had to start somewhere.

1838: The Grand Caledonian Curling Club is formed. Because of Scotland's growing interest in curling in the 19th century and a need for an official headquarters, John Cairnie, an experienced curler and builder of a curling hall in Largs, Scotland, sends out the call in 1833 for all Scottish clubs to submit lists of their officers, members and matches played. As a result of this compilation of statistics on Scotland's curlers, the "Mother Club of Curling" is born in Edinburgh, and the Grand Caledonian becomes the head club for curlers worldwide. Records have been kept of the club's members and their games since 1839 in a log called The Annuals.

1840: To avoid the harsh cold of the winter, the rest of the bigger curling clubs in Canada choose to build indoor rinks in which to curl.

(circa) 1840: The in-turns and out-turns of curling that caused such a fervour in Scotland in the late 18th century make their way to Canada, with decidedly less hubbub in the annals of curling history.

1841: The game of curling is standardized in Canada when Québec clubs join with the Grand Caledonian Curling Club back in Scotland. Named the Canadian Branch, Canadian curlers now have a bona fide connection with the Mother Club across the pond. All aspects of curling become standard except for, somewhat curiously, the use of both granite and iron stones, a practice that continues for approximately another 10 years.

1842: The Earl of Mansfield, president of the Grand Caledonian Curling Club, entertains Queen Victoria and Prince Albert on a visit to Scone Palace in Scotland by giving a demonstration of the game of curling on the hardwood floor of the Long Hall. The Earl also gives Prince Albert two Ailsa Craig stones (see 1973) and invites him to become the first patron of the Grand Caledonian Curling Club.

1843: Inspired by her visit to Scone Palace and Prince Albert's invitation, Queen Victoria grants permission to the Grand Caledonian Curling Club to change its name to the Royal Caledonian Curling Club as the Prince accepts his offer of patronage with the club. Curling history often calls this event the most prominent in the sport's history.

(circa) 1850: Iron stones are on their way out, and granite becomes the preferred stone in Canada. Colder winters on the Canadian Prairies result in deeper ice (therefore allowing deeper holes to be dug), which spurs the use of hacks. As a result, the precursor to the hack, the cram-pit (an iron footboard laid on the ice or attached to players' shoes), is also on its way out.

1858: The Canadian branch of the Royal Caledonian Curling Club in Montréal invites the Scots to tour Canada in a curling tournament. Scotland accepts the invitation, but their trip is put off for 44 years.

1865: The first international curling match takes place in Buffalo, U.S.A.—but only involves two countries, Canada and the United States. Twenty-three teams from each country participate, with Canada winning 658–478.

(circa) 1870: J.S. Russell, a native Scotsman living in Toronto and an avid curler, invents the type of standard curling stones still in use today. After submitting his ideal design to the primary manufacturer of curling stones in Scotland (Andrew Kay), Russell's stone, with its concave bottom and narrow running surface, is an instant and lasting success.

1873, 1876: Countries other than Scotland, Canada and the U.S. become involved in the sport of curling. Documented curling games take place in 1873 in Moscow, Russia, and in 1876 in St. Petersburg, Russia. However, curling does not fully catch on in Russia until over a century later in 1991.

1876: Winnipeg, Manitoba, forms its first curling club—a place that is destined to become the hub of curling not only in Canada but worldwide as well. On December 11, 1876, the first curling match is held in Winnipeg, and according to the custom of the time, the losers donate a barrel of oatmeal to the hospital.

1889: The first Winnipeg Bonspiel is held. Until the Brier begins in the early 20th century, Winnipeg's Bonspiel is the leading curling event in Canada.

1890s: Curling becomes more prevalent among women, with the formation of the Montréal Ladies Curling Club in 1894. It is said that this club was the first of its kind in the world, but as with many historical facts, there is no official document that confirms this. However, it is known that the Royal Caledonian Curling Club did not allow women in its ranks until 1895. The first

These Dawson City ladies represent the Yukon curling spirit, which originally came to the territory in 1898 when Scottish settlers arrived in droves for the Klondike Gold Rush.

women's group to join the Royal Caledonian club in that same year is the Hercules Club of Fifeshire.

1900: Patrons of the Royal Caledonian Curling Club are no longer just members of the Royal family—from this year on, they are either a king or queen exclusively.

1900: The first intercity bonspiel between women takes place with teams from Montréal and Québec City.

(circa) 1900: Curling clubs in Canada have almost all moved indoors to play out their matches, as ice-surfacing techniques get better and better.

1902: The long-delayed Scottish curling tour in North America finally begins its journey in Halifax, ending its Canadian leg in Winnipeg, and then venturing down to six cities in the U.S., ending the tour in New York. The entire tour takes about 40 days to complete.

(circa) early 1900s: The influence that a broom could have on a throw starts to become more interesting to curlers wanting to improve the game. Curlers discover that with skilled manipulation of the ordinary household brooms being used at the time, it is possible to increase the path and distance a stone can travel. Players now start to see the length of a rock's travel go up by 10 to 15 feet (3 to 4.5 metres), and sweepers can even delay the curl, depending on how ferociously they sweep and the condition of the ice surface. The rise of sweeping for line and distance becomes a new way to strategize in the game.

(circa) early 1900s: Bonspiels become the most popular form of competition in Canada.

1908: The first Canadian group of curlers make their way to Scotland, in reciprocation of the Scots' tour in Canada and the U.S. a few years earlier. The Canadian curlers win, claiming the Strathcona Cup.

1924: The oldest club in North America, the Montréal Curling Club, is given the privilege of adding "Royal" to the beginning of its name, cementing its link in history to the prestigious Royal Caledonian Curling Club.

1924: Curling becomes an Olympic medal sport at the first winter games in Chamonix, France. Only three countries represent curling at Chamonix—France, Great Britain and Sweden—and Great Britain takes gold.

1927: The famous Canadian men's Brier curling tournament is born. Named the Macdonald Brier because Macdonald Tobacco is the sponsor, it is the first national curling championship in Canada, and eight teams take part that inaugural year at the Granite Club in Toronto in a game that lasts 14 ends. "Brier" is also a brand of tobacco sold by the competition's sponsor.

1932: Curling is no longer a medal sport at the Lake Placid Olympics but is a demonstration sport, despite an increase in the number of teams entered—eight—with four from the U.S. and four from Canada. Winnipeg wins first place.

1935: A seemingly insignificant decision is made to trademark the Macdonald Tobacco brand of Export cigarettes with a Scottish girl wearing the Macdonald of Sleat tartan kilt. However, the "lassie" begins appearing on billboards in curling rinks because of the company's Brier sponsorship, and soon Macdonald's little Scottish girl becomes synonymous with the event and with curling.

1938: Even though curling is more popular than ever before, there is still a lack of uniformity in the rules of the game. In the Kilmarnock and Edinburgh areas, there are four players on each team, and each team member throws two stones. This method of play is deemed the most acceptable and becomes the standard with the Royal Caledonian Curling Club. The game is still played the same way today.

1940: The Brier shifts its location to Winnipeg, Manitoba, and for the first time, matched stones with coloured tops are used for easier identification.

1944: American Glenn Harris founds the *National Curling News*. The paper was renamed the *North American Curling News* in 1945, but was bought by the United States Curling Association in 1991 and renamed the *United States Curling News*.

1948: The U.S. Women's Curling Association is founded.

1948: The Macdonald Brier is broadcast on live radio by the Canadian Broadcasting Corporation, helping to make the event even more of a curling touchstone since its inception 21 years earlier.

1950: The precursor to what will set off professional curling for juniors is played in Canada: the first School Championship, with Saskatchewan's team taking first place.

(circa) 1950s: After World War II, people want to have fun, and curling clubs pop up everywhere. These clubs are better than any of the earlier ones, with improved freezing methods playing a central role in their construction.

The rinks are quite different from the stretch of uneven, possibly gritty ice on a backwoods creek that curlers used to play on. Builders excavate below the frost line and pour gravel and sand into a rink-size hole to create a level area free from frost heaving. Iron pipes through which refrigerant can flow are laid on wooden sleepers, and sand is poured on top to cover everything. The sand floor later gives way to a cement floor and eventually to a "floating" cement floor, which is a concrete slab with pipes inside of it that floats on a layer of insulation. After this is completed, the ice-maker goes to work. What a long way curlers had come since the 16th century!

(circa) 1950s: Mixed-gender curling becomes popular in the United States.

(circa) 1955: Up until this point, curlers in Québec and the Ottawa Valley in Canada hold fast to their use of iron stones. Their use of iron stones causes problems when organizing games and bonspiels with clubs that use granite stones. Helping to spur the change is the decision to amalgamate the Canadian Branch of the Royal Caledonian Curling Club with the Granite Curling Association.

1957: The first U.S. curling championship is held at Chicago Stadium, where the top curlers from 10 states play out this debut event.

1957: Curlers hold a meeting in Edinburgh to figure out how to form the necessary international committee needed to apply for Olympic medal status. Progress proves to be slow.

1958: Corn-straw brooms were popular for a while but make their way out quickly when it is discovered that inverting the straw in the centre of the broom (called the Blackjack, as coined by Fern Marchessault of Montréal) causes a very loud sound when swept and leaves debris all over the ice. "Keep it clean" becomes a curling phrase of the time.

1959: The Scotch Cup debuts in Scotland, which pits each country's national curling champions against one another. Canada wins, and by 1967, the Scotch Cup grows to an eight-country event, with the U.S. joining in 1961, Sweden in 1962, Norway and Switzerland in 1964, France in 1966 and Germany in 1967. Unfortunately, the Scotch Cup's final year is also 1967, but its creation eventually leads to the formation of the World Curling Championship, and the 1959–67 tournament results now count today as qualifying records in the history of the men's world championship.

(circa) 1963: Problems with brooms abound, and when Calgarian Ted Thonger creates the "Rink Rat" broom (a synthetic three-fingered broom), he boasts that it will no longer leave corn-straw bits on the ice, but players still had to deal with some cotton-covered plastic pieces that fell from the broom.

1965: Bud Somerville's U.S. team becomes the first non-Canadian foursome to win a world championship.

1965: Countries gather once again to form an international body to represent the sport of curling globally. Six countries (Scotland, Canada, U.S., Sweden, Norway and Switzerland) meet in Perth, Scotland, and under the Royal Caledonian Curling Club announce a new committee named the International Curling Federation (ICF). The federation makes its official constitution in Vancouver, British Columbia, in 1966, with France added to the original six countries making up the ICF. The federation eventually grows to be what it is today—the World Curling Federation—overseeing world championships for men, women, juniors, seniors, wheelchair curlers and mixed doubles.

1967 and 1968: With the demise of the Scotch Cup in 1967, the Air Canada Silver Broom takes its place at the 1968 World Curling Championship. From the get-go, eight countries compete in the Silver Broom until Italy and Denmark are added in 1973. The Worlds remain at 10 teams for almost 40 years, until the number allowed into the tournament goes up to 12 in 2005.

(circa) 1968: A pair of Calgary curlers tries out the horsehair broom of the Scots' liking and discovers a much more comfortable broom in comparison to the painful, blister-inducing corn-straw broom Canadian curlers used. A variety of brush heads, including hog's hair, horsehair and synthetic coverings, become available everywhere, and many are still in use today.

1972: Sponsor of the Brier, Macdonald Tobacco also supports the Canadian women's national championship (the Lassie), the first of which is played in 1972.

1973: Sweden's Kjell Oscarius' team wins the Air Canada Silver Broom—the first time a European rink takes a world curling title.

1973: The island of Ailsa Craig is famous in the world of curling because many granite stones are made from the rock found there— the hardest, purest, most dense granite available. Ailsa Craig granite is impervious to moisture, which in lesser quality granite causes the rock to freeze, expand and then expel the impurities, making the granite lumpy. And, as all curlers know, an imperfect surface just won't do. When curling was first introduced to the Royal family in 1842, Ailsa Craig stones were given to the Queen and the Prince as gifts, marking them as the best quality. The granite was readily available, seemingly never-ending, and in great supply—until the second half of the 20th century when obtaining the right rock from the island became increasingly expensive. Curling stones are made from large "blanks" or "cheeses" of granite, which have to be blasted out from the rock. Only one percent of all the rock blasted on Ailsa Craig produced blanks or cheeses big enough for curling stones, and so the entire operation on the island was shut down in 1973.

Ailsa Craig is now a bird sanctuary, but some of the island's stone still makes it into today's curling rocks. Modern manufacturers have created a process in which a small piece of Ailsa Craig granite can be inserted into an older rock to give it the smooth, coveted running surface of the old, treasured Ailsa Craig curling stones.

1974: Said to be the most deadly disaster to strike a curling club, a tornado blows through Windsor, Ontario, peeling the roof off the city's curling club while curlers are on the ice. Nine people are killed and many more are injured.

1975: The International Curling Federation endorses the World Junior Men's Curling Championship.

1977: The Grand Transatlantic Match begins in Karlstad, Sweden. The oceanic match-up admits Pacific curling nations shortly afterwards and is renamed the Grand Transoceanic Match (GTM). The GTM is modeled after Scotland's Great Match, which pits the north against the south. Unique to the GTM is that it allows spectator curlers from one side of the world to challenge spectators from the other side in a total points tournament. The dividing line changes every year, and one year in Garmisch-Partenkirchen, Germany, each game had to begin at midnight because organizers were honouring King Ludwig of Bavaria, who, oddly enough, would only travel at night.

1978: A new endurance record in curling is set when two British Columbia teams play for 61 hours and 20 minutes.

1979: The International Curling Federation endorses the Ladies' World Curling Championship, with the inaugural event taking place in Perth, Scotland.

1979: Macdonald Tobacco stops supporting the Lassie tournament, and therefore the event meets its demise. The tobacco company also withdraws its sponsorship of the Brier.

1980: Labatt takes over as sponsor of the Brier. The event itself is still going strong and switches tournament protocol to a playoff format following the preliminary round-robin games.

1982: The International Curling Federation is declared as independent and becomes the official governing body of curling throughout the world. However, the Royal Caledonian Curling Club is formally designated as the Mother Club of Curling, in recognition of its long history in the sport of curling.

1982: The first Scott Tournament of Hearts (the Canadian national women's championship) hits the ice in Regina, Saskatchewan, and curling star-to-be Colleen Jones of Nova Scotia wins. Jones goes on to win the Scott Tournament of Hearts in 1999, 2001 and 2002, earning her the distinction of being the first female skip to win four national titles. Jones went on to win a fifth and sixth time over the next two years.

1982: The first "Brier Patch" makes its debut. Mixing fans with the players in a community-like atmosphere, the Brier has always provided a common area for the two to mingle, but none as impressive as Don Pottinger's of Brandon, Manitoba. Named the

Brier Patch that first year, the "Patch," has been a mainstay at every Brier event since.

1982: A new curling endurance record in curling is set, beating the British Columbia teams from four years earlier: the *Guinness Book of Records* acknowledges two junior teams from Fredericton, New Brunswick, as the new record-holders, who played for 73 hours and 54 minutes.

1985: The final Air Canada Silver Broom world championship tournament is held in Glasgow, Scotland.

1986: The Air Canada Silver Broom may have ended in 1985, but in 1986 the world championships continue as Hexagon International is named the newest sponsor of the event. The first championship held under the Hexagon name is played in Toronto, Ontario. Canada's Ed Lukowich wins.

1988: Curling is a demonstration sport—yet again—at the Calgary Winter Olympics. Past president of the Canadian Curling Association and seasoned media personality Ray Kingsmith organizes the curling games, and despite a well laid-out plan and enthusiastic fans, the International Olympic Committee decides not to sanction curling as an official

Olympic medal sport. Canada's Linda Moore wins first place in the women's event (which is actually the first time women compete in curling at the Olympics, demonstration sport or not), and Norway's Eigil Ramsfjell wins in the men's event.

1988: Lasting only two years, the Hexagon-sponsored world championships come to an end in Lausanne, Switzerland. Norwegian Eigil Ramsfjell has a good year and wins this event as well.

1988: The International Curling Federation approves and supports the World Junior Ladies' Curling Championship.

1989: The ICF combines the men's and women's world championships into one event, sponsored by the federation. The inaugural event takes place in Milwaukee, Wisconsin. The junior men and women curlers are also included in this amalgamation.

1989: Because of the combination of the men's and women's world championships into one event, organizers fear the combined game activity of both genders will take up too much time. As a result, time clocks are introduced to the game and have been a fixture in top-level curling ever since.

1991: Safeway becomes the sponsor of the world championships.

1991: The International Curling Federation changes its name to the World Curling Federation because the name of another international federation causes some confusion—the International Canoeing Federation, also possessing the initials ICF.

1991: The Moncton 100 plays out its tournament, and as a bonspiel organized as a celebration of the New Brunswick city's civic centennial, it awards the largest amount of curling tournament prize money in the world at the time—$250,000. Also significant at the competition is the introduction of the Howard Rule to the game of curling. Named after its creator, Ontario's Russ Howard, the Howard Rule is modelled after one of its namesake's practice drills in which neither team was allowed to remove the first four stones of an end from play, whether in the rings or not. Players could move the rocks around, but could not remove them completely, a rule that proved to be popular.

1992: The Howard Rule is renamed the Free Guard Zone rule, and with one change, it is presented in play at the Albertville Olympics that same year. The modification for the

Olympics saw the Free Guard Zone restricted to an area between the hog line and the tee line outside the rings, whereas there was no restriction with the original Howard Rule. Also, while Canada opted for a three-rock Free Guard Zone rule, the rest of the world saw a four-rock rule to be the best choice for the game.

1992: Curling tries to be deemed an Olympic medal sport at the Albertville, France Winter Olympics, playing its games as a demonstration sport once again. Urs Dick of Switzerland wins the men's event, while Germany's Andrea Schopp takes the top spot in women's play.

1992: The Albertville games did the trick in that the International Olympic Committee in Barcelona finally grants curling the official designation of being a medal sport. Announced is the fact that curling will undoubtedly be awarded medals to its players at the 2002 Olympic Winter Games, but will be negotiable as a medal sport for the 1998 games, dependant on which city wins the bid. Curling is eventually accepted at Nagano, Japan, at the 1998 Winter Olympics, much to the delight of curlers everywhere.

1992: The first World Curling Tour tournament is played. This tour showcases the talents of the best curlers in the world through various bonspiels in different locations around the globe.

1992: The World Curling Players' Association is formed, with Ed Lukowich—longtime curler and winner of the 1986 Hexagon World Championship—as president.

1993: Safeway withdraws sponsorship of the World Curling Championships, and the World Curling Federation once again becomes the sponsor.

1994: Ford Canada is named as the new sponsor of the World Curling Championships.

1995: The first world curling championship is played under its new sponsor, Ford Canada, in Brandon, Manitoba. Kerry Burtnyk of Canada wins the men's title, while Sweden's Elisabet Gustafson takes the trophy in the women's tournament.

1998: The Nagano Winter Olympics host the long-awaited and newly named medal sport of curling. Canada (Sandra Schmirler) wins gold in the women's event, and Switzerland (Patrick Hurlimann) takes the men's event.

2000: Senior curlers play in an exhibition series at the World Championships in Glasgow, Scotland.

2000: The World Curling Federation moves its head offices from Perth, Scotland, to Edinburgh.

2001: The Grand Slam of Curling for men begins with events in Wainwright, Alberta, Gander, Newfoundland and Sault Ste. Marie, Ontario. The $100,000 cashspiels are completed with the World Curling Tour Players' Championship in Strathroy, Ontario.

2001: Nokia is the new sponsor of the Brier.

2002: The Continental Cup debuts in Regina, Saskatchewan. The event sees six world teams chosen by the World Curling Federation go head to head against six North American teams, as selected by the Canadian Curling Association and the U.S. branch.

2002: After exhibiting at the Worlds in 2000, the World Senior Championships are an official addition to the world championship tournament, including both men and women. At the inaugural addition to the Ford Worlds in Bismarck, North Dakota, Canada's Anne Dunn wins gold, as does American Larry Johnston for the the men's event.

2002: The World Curling Federation accepts wheelchair curling as an official sport, and the first World Wheelchair Curling Championship takes place in Sursee, Switzerland.

2002: The Olympic Winter Games are held in Salt Lake City, Utah. Pal Trulsenv from Norway wins the gold medal in men's curling, and Briton Rhona Martin takes the top spot in the women's event.

2002: During the Salt Lake City Winter Olympics, David Letterman airs a top-10 list on how to make curling "more exciting" after the event is, some curling naysayers might opine, overly broadcasted at the Olympics.

2002: The Canadian movie *Men with Brooms* debuts in theatres and grosses $1,040,000, proving that the passion for curling is alive and well. The movie had the largest opening weekend of all time (as of 2002) for a made-in-Canada English-language feature film in a national release.

2003: The USA Curling National Championships are aired for one hour on NBC, marking the first time this type of broadcast is seen on a national U.S. network.

2003: Scotland sends touring curling teams to Canada 100 years after the end of the original tour by the Scots in 1902–03.

2003: For the first time, curling claims a place at the World University Winter Games and at the Asian Winter Games.

2004: It is announced that Tim Hortons, beginning in 2005, will be the new sponsor of the Brier tournament.

2005: After playing together for 16 years, the men's and women's World Championships are separated again and held in different cities.

2005: The European Youth Olympic Festival announces it will count curling among its events, starting in 2005.

2006: The Turin Paralympic Games see the full-medal debut of wheelchair curling.

2006: The U.S. curling team wins their first Olympic medal (bronze) at the Turin Winter Games.

2006: The International Olympic Committee announces that the curling tournament at the 1924 Chamonix Olympics now counts as an officially sanctioned event in the history of the Olympics.

2006: Russia's women's team wins the Le Gruyère European Curling Championship.

The win marks the first time Russia earns a major curling title since its debut in international curling, circa 1992.

2007: Known as the Scott Tournament of Hearts since 1982, the name of the tournament gets changed to the Scotties Tournament of Hearts because of corporate takeovers.

2007: It is announced that the 2009 Ford Worlds will be held in Moncton, New Brunswick. This will be the championship's 50th anniversary and also the final tournament of the season for Member Associations of the World Curling Federation to earn their points in qualifying their countries for the 2010 Vancouver Olympics.

2008: The Pacific region wins its first world championship medal when Japan's Moe Meguro defeats Denmark in a tiebreaker at the Ford Worlds.

2008: Finland hosts the first World Mixed Doubles Curling Championship. Switzerland wins.

2008: The Sports Network (TSN) announces that, for the first time ever, they will televise the finals of the Ford World Championships, the Tim Hortons Brier, and the Scotties Tournament of Hearts in the 2009 season.

2008: The Continental Cup series will be held in Camrose, Alberta, in December, and the skips at the helm of Team North America will be Kevin Martin (Canada) Jennifer Jones (Canada), Craig Brown (U.S.), Debbie McCormick (U.S.), Kevin Koe (Canada) and Stefanie Lawton (Canada). Team World will include skips Anette Norberg of Sweden, David Murdoch of Scotland, two teams from China (Bingyu Wang and Fengchun Wang), Switzerland's Mirjam Ott and Norway's Thomas Ulsrud.

2008: The Canadian Curling Association (CCA) announces that Iqaluit, Nunavut, will host the 2009 Canadian Mixed Curling Championship. The CCA is the first sport association to assign a national championship in either summer or winter in Nunavut.

2009: The World Junior Championship will be played at the new Hillcrest/Nat Bailey Stadium Park in Vancouver; this event will act as a test tournament in the lead-up to the 2010 Olympics.

2010: Looking ahead to the Vancouver Winter Olympic Games, the curling events will take place at Hillcrest/Nat Bailey Stadium Park—which will be built by the end of 2008—and will follow the same game format used four years earlier at the Turin Games: 10 teams play a round-robin tournament, from which the top four teams go on to the semi-finals. As the host country, Canada's men's and women's teams qualify automatically for the curling competition.

The Stats

Key

G = Gold

S = Silver

B = Bronze

P = Position

L = Lead

2 = Second

3 = Third

S = Skip

% = Shot percentage

W = Win

L = Loss

R = Ranking

Men's European Curling Championships

Year	Country	Team
2007	Scotland	David Murdoch (S), Graeme Connal, Peter Smith, Euan Byers, David Hay
2006	Switzerland	Andi Schwaller (S), Ralph Stöckli, Thomas Lips, Damian Grichting
2005	Norway	Pål Trulsen (S), Lars Vågberg, Flemming Davanger, Bent Ånund Ramsfjell, Torger Nergård
2004	Germany	Sebastian Stock (S), Daniel Herberg, Stephan Knoll, Markus Messenzehl, Patrick Hoffman
2003	Scotland	David Murdoch (S), Craig Wilson, Neil Murdoch, Euan Byers, Ronald Brewster
2002	Germany	Sebastian Stock (S), Daniel Herberg, Stephan Knoll, Markus Messenzehl, Patrick Hoffman
2001	Sweden	Peja Lindholm (S), Tomas Nordin, Magnus Swartling, Peter Narup, Anders Kraupp
2000	Finland	Markku Uusipaavalniemi (S), Wille Mäkelä, Tommi Häti, Jari Laukkanen, Pekka Saarelainen
1999	Scotland	Hammy McMillan (S), Warwick Smith, Ewan MacDonald, Peter Loudon, James Dryburgh
1998	Sweden	Peja Lindholm (S), Tomas Nordin, Magnus Swartling, Peter Narup, Joakim Carlsson
1997	Germany	Andy Kapp (S), Uli Kapp, Oliver Axnick, Holger Höhne, Michael Schäffer
1996	Scotland	Hammy McMillan (S), Norman Brown, Mike Hay, Brian Binnie, Peter Loudon
1995	Scotland	Hammy McMillan (S), Norman Brown, Mike Hay, Roger McIntyre, Brian Binnie
1994	Scotland	Hammy McMillan (S), Norman Brown, Mike Hay, Roger McIntyre, Gordon Muirhead
1993	Norway	Eigil Ramsfjell (S), Sjur Loen, Dagfinn Loen, Niclas Järund, Espen de Lange
1992	Germany	Andy Kapp (S), Uli Kapp, Michael Schäffer, Oliver Axnick, Holger Höhne
1991	Germany	Roland Jentsch (S), Uli Sutor, Charlie Kapp, Alexander Huchel, Uli Kapp

Men's European Curling Championships, continued

Year	Country	Team
1990	Sweden	Mikael Hasselborg (S), Hans Nordin, Lars Vågberg, Stefan Hasselborg
1989	Scotland	Hammy McMillan (S), Norman Brown, Hugh Aitken, Jim Cannon
1988	Scotland	David Smith (S), Mike Hay, Peter Smith, David Hay
1987	Sweden	Thomas Norgren (S), Jan Strandlund, Lars Strandqvist, Lars Engblom, Olle Håkansson
1986	Switzerland	Felix Luchsinger (S), Thomas Grendelmeier, Daniel Steiff, Fritz Luchsinger
1985	Germany	Rodger Gustaf Schmidt (S), Wolfgang Burba, Johnny Jahr, Hans-Joachim Burba
1984	Switzerland	Peter Attinger Jr. (S), Bernhard Attinger, Werner Attinger, Kurt Attinger
1983	Switzerland	Amédéé Biner (S), Walter Bielser, Alex Aufdenblatten, Alfred Paci
1982	Scotland	Mike Hay (S), David Hay, David Smith, Russell Keiller
1981	Switzerland	Jürg Tanner (S), Jürg Hornisberger, Patrik Lörtscher, Franz Tanner
1980	Scotland	Barton Henderson (S), Greig Henderson, Bill Henderson, Alistair Sinclair
1979	Scotland	Jimmy Waddell (S), Willie Frame, Jim Forrest, George Bryan
1978	Switzerland	Jürg Tanner (S), Jürg Hornisberger, Franz Tanner, Patrik Lörtscher
1977	Sweden	Ragnar Kamp (S), Björn Rudström, Håkan Rudström, Christer Mårtensson
1976	Switzerland	Peter Attinger Jr. (S), Bernhard Attinger, Mattias Neuen-schwander, Ruedi Attinger
1975	Norway	Knut Bjaanaes (S), Sven Kroken, Helmer Strømbo, Kjell Ulrichsen

Women's European Curling Championships

Year	Country	Team
2007	Sweden	Anette Norberg (S), Eva Lund, Cathrine Lindahl, Anna Svärd, Maria Prytz
2006	Russia	Ludmila Privivkova (S), Olga Jarkova, Nkeirouka Ezekh, Ekaterina Galkina
2005	Sweden	Anette Norberg (S), Eva Lund, Cathrine Lindahl, Anna Bergström, Ulrika Bergman
2004	Sweden	Anette Norberg (S), Eva Lund, Cathrine Norberg, Anna Bergström, Ulrika Bergman
2003	Sweden	Anette Norberg (S), Eva Lund, Cathrine Norberg, Anna Bergström, Maria Prytz
2002	Sweden	Anette Norberg (S), Cathrine Norberg, Eva Lund, Helena Lingham, Maria Hasselborg
2001	Sweden	Anette Norberg (S), Cathrine Norberg, Eva Lund, Maria Hasselborg, Anna Rindeskog
2000	Sweden	Elisabet Gustafson (S), Katarina Nyberg, Louise Marmont, Elisabeth Persson, Christina Bertrup
1999	Norway	Dordi Nordby (S), Hanne Woods, Marianne Aspelin, Cecilie Torhaug
1998	Germany	Andrea Schöpp (S), Natalie Neßler, Heike Wieländer, Jane Boake-Cope, Andrea Stock
1997	Sweden	Elisabet Gustafson (S), Katarina Nyberg, Louise Marmont, Elisabeth Persson, Margaretha Lindahl
1996	Switzerland	Mirjam Ott (S), Marianne Flotron, Franziska von Känel, Caroline Balz, Annina von Planta
1995	Germany	Andrea Schöpp (S), Monika Wagner, Natalie Neßler, Carina Meidele, Heike Wieländer
1994	Denmark	Helena Blach Lavrsen (S), Dorthe Holm, Margit Pörtner, Helene Jensen, Lisa Richardson
1993	Sweden	Elisabet Johansson (S), Katarina Nyberg, Louise Marmont, Elisabeth Persson, Eva Eriksson
1992	Sweden	Elisabet Johansson (S), Katarina Nyberg, Louise Marmont, Elisabeth Persson
1991	Germany	Andrea Schöpp (S), Stephanie Mayer, Monika Wagner, Sabine Huth

Women's European Curling Championships, continued

Year	Country	Team
1990	Norway	Dordi Nordby (S), Hanne Pettersen, Mette Halvorsen, Anne Jøtun
1989	Germany	Andrea Schöpp (S), Monika Wagner, Christina Haller, Heike Wieländer
1988	Sweden	Elisabeth Högström (S), Anette Norberg, Monika Jansson, Marie Henriksson
1987	Germany	Andrea Schöpp (S), Almut Hege, Monika Wagner, Suzanne Fink
1986	Germany	Andrea Schöpp (S), Almut Hege, Monika Wagner, Elinore Schöpp
1985	Switzerland	Jaqueline Landolt (S), Christine Krieg, Marianne Uhlmann, Silvia Benoit
1984	Germany	Almut Hege (S), Josefine Einsle, Suzanne Koch, Petra Tschetsch
1983	Sweden	Elisabeth Högström (S), Katarina Hultling, Birgitta Sewik, Karin Sjögren
1982	Sweden	Elisabeth Högström (S), Katarina Hultling, Birgitta Sewik, Karin Sjögren
1981	Switzerland	Susan Schlapbach (S), Irene Bürgi, Ursula Schlapbach, Katrin Peterhans
1980	Sweden	Elisabeth Högström (S), Carina Olsson, Birgitta Sewik, Karin Sjögren
1979	Switzerland	Gaby Casanova (S), Betty Bourquin, Linda Thommen, Rosi Manger
1978	Sweden	Inga Arfwidsson (S), Barbro Arfwidsson, Ingrid Appelquist, Gunvor Björhäll
1977	Sweden	Elisabeth Branäs (S), Eva Rosenhed, Britt-Marie Ericson, Anne-Marie Ericsson
1976	Sweden	Elisabeth Branäs (S), Elisabeth Högström, Eva Rosenhed, Anne-Marie Ericsson
1975	Scotland	Betty Law (S), Jessie Whiteford, Beth Lindsay, Isobel Ross

Olympic Winter Games — Men's

Year	Medal	Country	Team
2006	G	Canada	Russ Howard (S), Brad Gushue, Mark Nichols, Jamie Korab, Mike Adam
	S	Finland	Markku Uusipaavalniemi (S), Wille Mäkelä, Kalle Kiiskinen, Teemu Salo, Jani Sullanmaa
	B	United States	Pete Fenson (S), Shawn Rojeski, Joseph Polo, John Shuster, Scott Baird
2002	G	Norway	Pål Trulsen (S), Lars Vågberg, Flemming Davanger, Bent Ånund Ramsfjell, Torger Nergård
	S	Canada	Kevin Martin (S), Don Walchuk, Carter Rycroft, Don Bartlett, Ken Tralnberg
	B	Switzerland	Andreas Schwaller (S), Christof Schwaller, Markus Eggler, Damian Grichting, Marco Ramstein
1998	G	Switzerland	Patrick Hürlimann (S), Patrik Lörtscher, Daniel Müller, Diego Perren, Dominic Andres
	S	Canada	Mike Harris (S), Richard Hart, Collin Mitchell, George Karrys, Paul Savage
	B	Norway	Eigil Ramsfjell (S), Jan Thoresen, Stig-Arne Gunnestad, Anthon Grimsmo, Tore Torvbråten
1924	G	Great Britain	Willie K. Jackson (S), Robin Welsh, Tom B. Murray, Laurence Jackson, John T. Robertson Aikman
	S	Sweden	Carl Wilhelm Petersén (S), Ture Ödlund, Victor Wetterström, Erik Severin
	S	Sweden	Johan Petter Åhlén (S), Carl-Axel Pettersson, Karl-Erik Wahlberg, Carl Axel Kronlund
	B	France	F. Cournollet (S), P. Canivet, A. Benedic, G. André

Olympic Winter Games — Women's

Year	Medal	Country	Team
2006	G	Sweden	Anette Norberg (S), Eva Lund, Cathrine Lindahl, Anna Svärd, Ulrika Bergman
	S	Switzerland	Mirjam Ott (S), Binia Beeli, Valeria Spälty, Michèle Moser, Manuela Kormann
	B	Canada	Shannon Kleibrink (S), Amy Nixon, Glenys Bakker, Christine Keshen, Sandra Jenkins
2002	G	Great Britain	Rhona Martin (S), Deborah Knox, Fiona MacDonald, Janice Rankin, Margaret Morton
	S	Switzerland	Luzia Ebnöther (S), Mirjam Ott, Tanya Frei, Laurence Bidaud, Nadia Röthlisberger
	B	Canada	Kelley Law (S), Julie Skinner, Georgina Wheatcroft, Diane Nelson, Cheryl Noble
1998	G	Canada	Sandra Schmirler (S), Jan Betker, Joan McCusker, Marcia Gudereit, Atina Ford
	S	Denmark	Helena Blach Lavrsen (S), Margit Pörtner, Dorthe Holm, Trine Qvist, Jane Bidstrup
	B	Sweden	Elisabet Gustafson (S), Katarina Nyberg, Louise Marmont, Elisabeth Persson, Margaretha Lindahl

Scott ("Scotties" as of 2007) Tournament of Hearts

2008

FINAL

Team	1	2	3	4	5	6	7	8	9	10	11	Total
Alberta	0	1	0	2	0	1	0	0	0	0	x	4
Manitoba	0	0	2	0	2	0	0	1	0	1	x	6

P	Alberta	%
L	Chelsey Bell	94
2	Bronwen Saunders	81
3	Amy Nixon	74
S	Shannon Kleibrink	76

P	Manitoba	%
L	Dawn Askin	91
2	Jill Officer	89
3	Cathy Overton-Clapham	89
S	Jennifer Jones	86

SEMI-FINAL

Team	1	2	3	4	5	6	7	8	9	10	11	Total
Ontario	1	0	0	0	3	0	2	0	2	0	0	8
Manitoba	0	2	1	1	0	2	0	1	0	1	1	9

P	Ontario	%
L	Andra Harmark	83
2	Kim Moore	84
3	Kirsten Wall	89
S	Sherry Middaugh	66

P	Manitoba	%
L	Dawn Askin	93
2	Jill Officer	84
3	Cathy Overton-Clapham	81
S	Jennifer Jones	83

Round-robin Standings

Team	W	L
Alberta	10	1
Ontario	9	2
Québec	8	3
Manitoba	7	4
Newfoundland & Labrador	7	4
Nova Scotia	6	5

Team	W	L
Saskatchewan	5	6
Canada	5	6
British Columbia	4	7
Prince Edward Island	3	8
Northwest Territories & Yukon	1	10
New Brunswick	1	10

Scott ("Scotties" as of 2007) Tournament of Hearts, continued

2007

FINAL

Team	1	2	3	4	5	6	7	8	9	10	Total
Canada	2	2	0	2	0	0	1	1	0	x	8
Saskatchewan	0	0	1	0	1	1	0	0	2	x	5

P	Canada	%
L	Renee Simons	72
2	Sasha Carter	79
3	Jeanna Schraeder	89
S	Kelly Scott	82

P	Saskatchewan	%
L	Marcia Gudereit	88
2	Nancy Inglis	64
3	Lana Vey	80
S	Jan Betker	74

SEMI-FINAL

Team	1	2	3	4	5	6	7	8	9	10	Total
Canada	2	1	1	0	1	0	1	0	1	x	7
Manitoba	0	0	0	1	0	2	0	2	0	x	5

P	Canada	%
L	Renee Simons	80
2	Sasha Carter	81
3	Jeanna Schraeder	81
S	Kelly Scott	83

P	Manitoba	%
L	Janet Arnott	89
2	Jill Officer	63
3	Cathy Overton-Clapham	69
S	Jennifer Jones	64

Round-robin Standings

Team	W	L
Canada	10	1
Saskatchewan	9	2
Manitoba	9	2
Prince Edward Island	6	5
Alberta	6	5
Ontario	6	5

Team	W	L
Newfoundland & Labrador	5	6
British Columbia	5	6
Québec	4	7
Nova Scotia	3	8
Northwest Territories & Yukon	2	9
New Brunswick	1	10

Scott ("Scotties" as of 2007) Tournament of Hearts, continued

2006

FINAL

Team	1	2	3	4	5	6	7	8	9	10	Total
British Columbia	1	0	3	1	0	1	1	0	0	1	8
Canada	0	1	0	0	2	0	0	2	1	0	6

P	British Columbia	%
L	Renee Simons	66
2	Sasha Carter	85
3	Jeanna Schraeder	86
S	Kelly Scott	82

P	Canada	%
L	Georgina Wheatcroft	98
2	Jill Officer	79
3	Cathy Overton-Clapham	80
S	Jennifer Jones	75

SEMI-FINAL

Team	1	2	3	4	5	6	7	8	9	10	Total
Nova Scotia	1	0	1	0	1	0	1	0	x	x	4
Canada	0	2	0	1	0	3	0	4	x	x	10

P	Nova Scotia	%
L	Nancy Delahunt	92
2	Mary-Anne Arsenault	89
3	Kim Kelly	83
S	Colleen Jones	63

P	Canada	%
L	Georgina Wheatcroft	83
2	Jill Officer	77
3	Cathy Overton-Clapham	78
S	Jennifer Jones	91

Round-robin Standings

Team	W	L
British Columbia	9	2
Nova Scotia	8	3
Canada	8	3
Québec	7	4
Newfoundland & Labrador	7	4
Alberta	6	5

Team	W	L
New Brunswick	5	6
Manitoba	4	7
Prince Edward Island	4	7
Ontario	4	7
Northwest Territories & Yukon	2	9
Saskatchewan	2	9

Scott ("Scotties" as of 2007) Tournament of Hearts, continued

2005

FINAL

Team	1	2	3	4	5	6	7	8	9	10	Total
Manitoba	0	0	2	0	0	0	1	1	0	4	8
Ontario	0	2	0	1	1	1	0	0	1	0	6

P	Manitoba	%
L	Cathy Gauthier	86
2	Jill Officer	75
3	Cathy Overton-Clapham	76
S	Jennifer Jones	70

P	Ontario	%
L	Steph Hanna	78
2	Dawn Askin	88
3	Pascale Letendre	75
S	Jenn Hanna	80

SEMI-FINAL

Team	1	2	3	4	5	6	7	8	9	10	Total
British Columbia	1	0	3	0	1	0	1	0	1	0	7
Ontario	0	2	0	1	0	2	0	2	0	2	9

P	British Columbia	%
L	Renee Simons	94
2	Sasha Carter	84
3	Michelle Allen	79
S	Kelly Scott	73

P	Ontario	%
L	Steph Hanna	94
2	Dawn Askin	84
3	Pascale Letendre	93
S	Jenn Hanna	86

Round-robin Standings

Team	W	L
Manitoba	9	2
British Columbia	8	3
Saskatchewan	7	4
Ontario	6	5
Alberta	6	5
Canada	6	5

Team	W	L
New Brunswick	6	5
Nova Scotia	5	6
Québec	4	7
Northwest Territories & Yukon	4	7
Prince Edward Island	4	7
Newfoundland & Labrador	1	10

Scott ("Scotties" as of 2007) Tournament of Hearts — Winners

Year	Team	Members
2008	Manitoba	Jennifer Jones (S), Dawn Askin, Jill Officer, Cathy Overton-Clapham
2007	Canada	Kelly Scott (S), Renee Simons, Sasha Carter, Jeanna Schraeder
2006	British Columbia	Kelly Scott (S), Renee Simons, Sasha Carter, Jeanna Schraeder
2005	Manitoba	Jennifer Jones (S), Cathy Gauthier, Jill Officer, Cathy Overton-Clapham
2004	Canada	Colleen Jones (S), Kim Kelly, Mary-Anne Arsenault, Nancy Delahunt
2003	Canada	Colleen Jones (S), Kim Kelly, Mary-Anne Waye, Nancy Delahunt
2002	Canada	Colleen Jones (S), Kim Kelly, Mary-Anne Waye, Nancy Delahunt
2001	Nova Scotia	Colleen Jones (S), Kim Kelly, Mary-Anne Waye, Nancy Delahunt
2000	British Columbia	Kelley Law (S), Julie Skinner, Georgina Wheatcroft, Diane Nelson
1999	Nova Scotia	Colleen Jones (S), Kim Kelly, Mary-Anne Waye, Nancy Delahunt
1998	Alberta	Cathy Borst (S), Heather Godberson, Brenda Bohmer, Kate Horne
1997	Saskatchewan	Sandra Schmirler (S), Jan Betker, Joan McCusker, Marcia Gudereit
1996	Ontario	Marilyn Bodogh (S), Kim Gellard, Corie Beveridge, Jane Hooper Perroud
1995	Manitoba	Connie Laliberte (S), Cathy Overton, Cathy Gauthier, Janet Arnott
1994	Canada	Sandra Peterson (S), Jan Betker, Joan McCusker, Marcia Gudereit
1993	Saskatchewan	Sandra Peterson (S), Jan Betker, Joan McCusker, Marcia Gudereit

Scott ("Scotties" as of 2007) Tournament of Hearts — Winners, continued

Year	Team	Members
1992	Manitoba	Connie Laliberte (S), Laurie Allen, Cathy Gauthier, Janet Arnott
1991	British Columbia	Julie Sutton (S), Jodie Sutton, Melissa Soligo, Karri Willms
1990	Ontario	Alison Goring (S), Kristin Turcotte, Andrea Lawes, Cheryl McPherson
1989	Canada	Heather Houston (S), Lorraine Lang, Diane Adams, Tracy Kennedy
1988	Ontario	Heather Houston (S), Lorraine Lang, Diane Adams, Tracy Kennedy
1987	British Columbia	Pat Sanders (S), Louise Herlinveaux, Georgina Hawkes, Deb Massullo
1986	Ontario	Marilyn Darte (S), Kathy McEdwards, Chris Jurgenson, Jan Augustyn
1985	British Columbia	Linda Moore (S), Lindsay Sparkes, Debbie Jones, Laurie Carney
1984	Manitoba	Connie Laliberte (S), Chris More, Corinne Peters, Janet Arnott
1983	Nova Scotia	Penny Larocque (S), Sharon Horne, Cathy Caudle, Pam Sanford
1982	Nova Scotia	Colleen Jones (S), Kay Smith, Monica Jones, Barbara Jones-Gordon
1981	Alberta	Susan Seitz (S), Judy Erickson, Myrna McKay, Betty McCracken
1980	Saskatchewan	Marj Mitchell (S), Nancy Kerr, Shirley McKendry, Wendy Leach
1979	British Columbia	Lindsay Sparkes (S), Dawn Knowles, Robin Wilson, Lorraine Bowles
1978	Manitoba	Cathy Pidzarko (S), Chris Pidzarko, Iris Armstrong, Patty Vanderkerckhove
1977	Alberta	Myrna McQuarrie (S), Rita Tarnava, Barb Davis, Jane Rempel

Scott ("Scotties" as of 2007) Tournament of Hearts — Winners, continued

Year	Team	Members
1976	British Columbia	Lindsay Davie (S), Dawn Knowles, Robin Wilson, Lorraine Bowles
1975	Québec	Lee Tobin (S), Marilyn McNeil, Michelle Garneau, Laurie Ross
1974	Saskatchewan	Emily Farnham (S), Linda Saunders, Pat McBeath, Donna Collins
1973	Saskatchewan	Vera Pezer (S), Sheila Rowan, Joyce McKee, Lenore Morrison
1972	Saskatchewan	Vera Pezer (S), Sheila Rowan, Joyce McKee, Lenore Morrison
1971	Saskatchewan	Vera Pezer (S), Sheila Rowan, Joyce McKee, Lenore Morrison
1970	Saskatchewan	Dorenda Schoenhals (S), Cheryl Stirton, Linda Burnham, Joan Anderson
1969	Saskatchewan	Joyce McKee (S), Vera Pezer, Lenore Morrison, Jennifer Falk
1968	Alberta	Hazel Jamison (S), Gale Lee, Jackie Spencer, June Coyle
1967	Manitoba	Betty Duguid (S), Joan Ingram, Larie Bradawaski, Dot Rose
1966	Alberta	Gale Lee (S), Hazel Jamison, Sharon Harrington, June Coyle
1965	Manitoba	Peggy Casselman (S), Val Taylor, Pat MacDonald, Pat Scott
1964	British Columbia	Ina Hansen (S), Ada Callas, Isabel Leith, May Shaw
1963	New Brunswick	Mabel DeWare (S), Harriet Stratton, Forbis Stevenson, Marjorie Fraser
1962	British Columbia	Ina Hansen (S), Ada Callas, Isabel Leith, May Shaw
1961	Saskatchewan	Joyce McKee (S), Sylvia Fedoruk, Barbara MacNevin, Rosa McFee

The Brier

2008

FINAL

Team	1	2	3	4	5	6	7	8	9	10	11	Total
Alberta	0	1	0	2	0	1	0	0	0	1	x	5
Ontario	0	0	1	0	1	0	0	0	2	0	x	4

P	Alberta	%
L	Ben Hebert	78
2	Marc Kennedy	84
3	John Morris	90
S	Kevin Martin	79

P	Ontario	%
L	Craig Savill	89
2	Brent Laing	80
3	Richard Hart	80
S	Glenn Howard	83

SEMI-FINAL

Team	1	2	3	4	5	6	7	8	9	10	11	Total
Saskatchewan	0	1	0	1	0	1	0	3	0	1	0	7
Ontario	0	0	2	0	2	0	2	0	1	0	1	8

P	Saskatchewan	%
L	Steve Laycock	84
2	Gerry Adam	76
3	Jeff Sharp	77
S	Pat Simmons	80

P	Ontario	%
L	Craig Savill	90
2	Brent Laing	77
3	Richard Hart	95
S	Glenn Howard	89

Round-robin Standings

Team	W	L
Alberta	11	0
Saskatchewan	9	2
Ontario	9	2
British Columbia	7	4
Newfoundland & Labrador	7	4
Manitoba	6	5

Team	W	L
Québec	4	7
Northern Ontario	3	8
Prince Edward Island	3	8
Nova Scotia	3	8
New Brunswick	2	9
Northwest Territories & Yukon	2	9

The Brier, continued

2007

FINAL

Team	1	2	3	4	5	6	7	8	9	10	Total
Nfld. & Labrador	0	2	0	2	1	0	0	1	0	x	6
Ontario	1	0	2	0	0	2	2	0	3	x	10

P	Newfoundland & Labrador	%
L	Jamie Korab	90
2	Chris Schille	75
3	Mark Nichols	88
S	Brad Gushue	86

P	Ontario	%
L	Craig Savill	88
2	Brent Laing	96
3	Richard Hart	90
S	Glenn Howard	83

SEMI-FINAL

Team	1	2	3	4	5	6	7	8	9	10	Total
Ontario	2	0	2	1	1	0	1	0	1	x	8
Manitoba	0	2	0	0	0	1	0	1	0	x	4

P	Ontario	%
L	Craig Savill	93
2	Brent Laing	89
3	Richard Hart	93
S	Glenn Howard	83

P	Manitoba	%
L	Steve Gould	90
2	Rob Fowler	81
3	Ryan Fry	79
S	Jeff Stoughton	74

Round-robin Standings

Team	W	L
Ontario	10	1
Newfoundland & Labrador	8	3
Manitoba	8	3
Alberta	8	3
Saskatchewan	7	4
Northern Ontario	5	6

Team	W	L
Northwest Territories & Yukon	5	6
British Columbia	4	7
Québec	4	7
Prince Edward Island	4	7
Nova Scotia	2	9
New Brunswick	1	10

The Brier, continued

2006

FINAL

Team	1	2	3	4	5	6	7	8	9	10	Total
Québec	1	3	0	1	0	2	0	1	0	0	8
Ontario	0	0	2	0	2	0	1	0	1	1	7

P	Québec	%
L	Maxime Elmaleh	90
2	Éric Sylvain	70
3	François Roberge	83
S	Jean-Michel Ménard	85

P	Ontario	%
L	Craig Savill	90
2	Brent Laing	81
3	Richard Hart	80
S	Glenn Howard	80

SEMI-FINAL

Team	1	2	3	4	5	6	7	8	9	10	Total
Québec	2	0	3	0	0	1	0	1	0	0	7
Nova Scotia	0	1	0	1	1	0	1	0	1	1	6

P	Québec	%
L	Maxime Elmaleh	90
2	Éric Sylvain	70
3	François Roberge	83
S	Jean-Michel Ménard	85

P	Nova Scotia	%
L	Andrew Gibson	91
2	Rob Harris	81
3	Bruce Lohnes	66
S	Mark Dacey	74

Round-robin Standings

Team	W	L
Ontario	10	1
Québec	8	3
Alberta	8	3
Nova Scotia	6	5
Northwest Territories & Yukon	7	4
Manitoba	7	4

Team	W	L
British Columbia	7	4
Saskatchewan	5	6
New Brunswick	5	6
Prince Edward Island	3	8
Newfoundland & Labrador	2	9
Northern Ontario	0	11

The Brier, continued

2005

FINAL

Team	1	2	3	4	5	6	7	8	9	10	Total
Alberta	1	0	1	0	1	1	0	0	0	1	5
Nova Scotia	0	2	0	1	0	0	0	1	0	0	4

P	Alberta	%
L	Marcel Rocque	84
2	Scott Pfeifer	88
S	Randy Ferbey	93
4	David Nedohin	88

P	Nova Scotia	%
L	Kelly Mittelstadt	88
2	Craig Burgess	90
3	Paul Flemming	80
S	Shawn Adams	81

SEMI-FINAL

Team	1	2	3	4	5	6	7	8	9	10	Total
Manitoba	0	2	0	1	1	0	1	0	1	1	7
Nova Scotia	1	0	4	0	0	2	0	1	0	0	8

P	Manitoba	%
L	Shane Kilgallen	84
2	Greg Melnichuk	60
3	Dave Elias	70
S	Randy Dutiame	73

P	Nova Scotia	%
L	Kelly Mittelstadt	74
2	Craig Burgess	88
3	Paul Flemming	83
S	Shawn Adams	84

Round-robin Standings

Team	W	L	Team	W	L
Alberta	9	2	Newfoundland & Labrador	6	5
Manitoba	8	3	Saskatchewan	6	5
Nova Scotia	8	3	Prince Edward Island	4	7
Québec	7	4	Northern Ontario	3	8
British Columbia	6	5	New Brunswick	3	8
Ontario	6	5	Northwest Territories & Yukon	0	11

The Brier Winners

Year	Team	Members
2008	Alberta	Kevin Martin (S), Ben Hebert, Marc Kennedy, John Morris
2007	Ontario	Glenn Howard (S), Craig Savill, Brent Laing, Richard Hart
2006	Québec	Jean-Michel Ménard (S), Maxime Elmaleh, Éric Sylvain, François Roberge
2005	Alberta	David Nedohin (S), Marcel Rocque, Scott Pfeifer, Randy Ferbey
2004	Nova Scotia	Mark Dacey (S), Bruce Lohnes, Rob Harris, Andrew Gibson
2003	Alberta	Randy Ferbey (S), David Nedohin, Scott Pfeifer, Marcel Rocque
2002	Alberta	Randy Ferbey (S), David Nedohin, Scott Pfeifer, Marcel Rocque
2001	Alberta	Randy Ferbey (S), David Nedohin, Scott Pfeifer, Marcel Rocque
2000	British Columbia	Greg McAulay (S), Brent Pierce, Bryan Miki, Jody Sveistrup
1999	Manitoba	Jeff Stoughton (S), Jon Mead, Garry VanDenBerghe, Doug Armstrong
1998	Ontario	Wayne Middaugh (S), Graeme McCarrel, Ian Tetley, Scott Bailey
1997	Alberta	Kevin Martin (S), Don Walchuk, Rudy Ramcharan, Don Bartlett
1996	Manitoba	Jeff Stoughton (S), Ken Tresoor, Garry VanDenBerghe, Steve Gould
1995	Manitoba	Kerry Burtnyk (S), Jeff Ryan, Rob Meakin, Keith Fenton
1994	British Columbia	Rick Folk (S), Pat Ryan, Bert Gretzinger, Gerry Richard
1993	Ontario	Russ Howard (S), Glenn Howard, Wayne Middaugh, Peter Corner
1992	Manitoba	Vic Peters (S), Dan Carey, Chris Neufeld, Don Rudd

The Brier Winners, continued

Year	Team	Members
1991	Alberta	Kevin Martin (S), Kevin Park, Dan Petryk, Don Barlett
1990	Ontario	Ed Werenich (S), John Kawaja, Ian Tetley, Pat Perroud
1989	Alberta	Pat Ryan (S), Randy Ferbey, Don Walchuk, Don McKenzie
1988	Alberta	Pat Ryan (S), Randy Ferbey, Don Walchuk, Don McKenzie
1987	Ontario	Russ Howard (S), Glenn Howard, Tim Belcourt, Kent Carstairs
1986	Alberta	Ed Lukowich (S), John Ferguson, Neil Houston, Brent Syme
1985	Northern Ontario	Al Hackner (S), Rick Lang, Ian Tetley, Pat Perroud
1984	Manitoba	Michael Riley (S), Brian Toews, John Helston, Russ Wookey
1983	Ontario	Ed Werenich (S), Paul Savage, John Kawaja, Neil Harrison
1982	Northern Ontario	Al Hackner (S), Rick Lang, Bob Nichol, Bruce Kennedy
1981	Manitoba	Kerry Burtnyk (S), Mark Olson, Jim Spencer, Ron Kammerlock
1980	Saskatchewan	Rick Folk (S), Ron Mills, Tom Wilson, Jim Wilson
1979	Manitoba	Barry Fry (S), Bill Carey, Gordon Sparkes, Bryan Wood
1978	Alberta	Ed Lukowich (S), Mike Chernoff, Dale Johnston, Ron Schindle
1977	Québec	Jim Ursel (S), Art Lobel, Don Aitken, Brian Ross
1976	Newfoundland	Jack Macduff (S), Toby Mcdonald, Doug Hudson, Ken Templeton
1975	Northern Ontario	Bill Tetley (S), Rick Lang, Bill Hodgson, Peter Hnatiw

The Brier Winners, continued

Year	Team	Members
1974	Alberta	Hec Gervais (S), Ron Anton, Warren Hansen, Darrel Sutton
1973	Saskatchewan	Harvey Mazinke (S), Billy Martin, George Achtymichuk, Dan Klippenstein
1972	Manitoba	Orest Meleschuk (S), Dave Romaro, John Hanesiak, Pat Hailley
1971	Manitoba	Don Duguid (S), Rod Hunter, Jim Pettapiece, Bryan Wood
1970	Manitoba	Don Duguid (S), Rod Hunter, Jim Pettapiece, Bryan Wood
1969	Alberta	Ron Northcott (S), Dave Gerlach, Bernie Sparkes, Fred Storey
1968	Alberta	Ron Northcott (S), Jim Shields, Bernie Sparkes, Fred Storey
1967	Ontario	Alf Phillips Jr. (S), John Ross, Ron Manning, Keith Reilly
1966	Alberta	Ron Northcott (S), George Finks, Bernie Sparkes, Fred Storey
1965	Manitoba	Terry Braunstein (S), Don Duguid, Ron Braunstein, Ray Turnbull
1964	British Columbia	Lyall Dagg (S), Leo Hebert, Fred Britton, Barry Naimark
1963	Saskatchewan	Ernie Richardson (S), Arnold Richardson, Garnet Richardson, Mel Perry
1962	Saskatchewan	Ernie Richardson (S), Arnold Richardson, Garnet Richardson, Wes Richardson
1961	Alberta	Hec Gervais (S), Ron Anton, Ray Werner, Wally Ursuliak
1960	Saskatchewan	Ernie Richardson (S), Arnold Richardson, Garnet Richardson, Wes Richardson
1959	Saskatchewan	Ernie Richardson (S), Arnold Richardson, Garnet Richardson, Wes Richardson
1958	Alberta	Matt Baldwin (S), Jack Geddes, Gordon Haynes, Bill Price

The Brier Winners, continued

Year	Team	Members
1957	Alberta	Matt Baldwin (S), Gordon Haynes, Art Kleinmeyer, Bill Price
1956	Manitoba	Billy Walsh (S), Al Langlois, Cy White, Andy McWilliams
1955	Saskatchewan	Garnet Campbell (S), Don Campbell, Glenn Campbell, Lloyd Campbell
1954	Alberta	Matt Baldwin (S), Glenn Gray, Pete Ferry, Jim Collins
1953	Manitoba	Ab Gowanlock (S), Jim Williams, Art Pollon, Russ Jackman
1952	Manitoba	Billy Walsh (S), Al Langlois, Andy McWilliams, John Watson
1951	Nova Scotia	Don Oyler (S), George Hanson, Fred Dyke, Wally Knock
1950	Northern Ontario	Tim Ramsay (S), Len Williamson, Bill Weston, Billy Kenny
1949	Manitoba	Ken Watson (S), Grant Watson, Lyle Dyker, Charles Read
1948	British Columbia	Frenchy D'Amour (S), Bob McGhie, Fred Wendell, Jim Mark
1947	Manitoba	Jimmy Welsh (S), Alex Welsh, Jack Reid, Harry Monk
1946	Alberta	Billy Rose (S), Bart Swelin, Austin Smith, George Crooks
1945		Cancelled due to World War II
1944		Cancelled due to World War II
1943		Cancelled due to World War II
1942	Manitoba	Ken Watson (S), Grant Watson, Charlie Scrymgeour, Jim Grant
1941	Alberta	Howard Palmer (S), Jack Lebeau, Art Gooder, Clare Webb

The Brier Winners, continued

Year	Team	Members
1940	Manitoba	Howard Wood (S), Ernie Pollard, Howard Wood, Jr., Roy Enman
1939	Ontario	Bert Hall (S), Perry Hall, Ernie Parkes, Cam Seagram
1938	Manitoba	Ab Gowanlock (S), Bung Cartwell, Bill McKnight, Tom Knight
1937	Alberta	Cliff Manahan (S), Wes Robinson, Ross Manahan, Lloyd McIntyre
1936	Manitoba	Ken Watson (S), Grant Watson, Marvin MacIntyre, Charles Kerr
1935	Ontario	Gordon Campbell (S), Don Campbell, Gord Coates, Duncan Campbell
1934	Manitoba	Leo Johnson (S), Lorne Stewart, Linc Johnson, Marno Frederickson
1933	Alberta	Cliff Manahan (S), Harold Deeton, Harold Wolfe, Bert Ross
1932	Manitoba	Jimmy Congalton (S), Howard Wood, Bill Noble, Harry Mawhinney
1931	Manitoba	Bob Gourlay (S), Ernie Pollard, Arnold Lockerbie, Ray Stewart
1930	Manitoba	Harold Wood (S), Jimmy Congalton, Victor Wood, Lionel Wood
1929	Manitoba	Gordon Hudson (S), Don Rollo, Ron Singbusch, Bill Grant
1928	Manitoba	Gordon Hudson (S), Sam Penwarden, Ron Singbush, Bill Grant
1927	Nova Scotia	Murray Macneill (S), Al MacInnes, Cliff Torey, Jim Donahoe

United States Curling Championships — Men's

Year	Team	Members
2008	Wisconsin	Craig Brown (S), Rich Ruohonen, John Dunlop, Pete Annis
2007	Minnesota	Todd Birr (S), Bill Todhunter, Greg Johnson, Kevin Birr
2006	Minnesota	Pete Fenson (S), Shawn Rojeski, Joe Polo, John Shuster, Scott Baird
2005	Minnesota	Pete Fenson (S), Shawn Rojeski, Joe Polo, John Shuster
2004	Washington	Jason Larway (S), Doug Pottinger, Joel Larway, Bill Todhunter, Doug Kauffman
2003	Minnesota	Pete Fenson (S), Eric Fenson, Shawn Rojeski, John Shuster
2002	Wisconsin	Paul Pustovar (S), Mike Fraboni, Geoff Goodland, Richard Maskel
2001	Washington	Jason Larway (S), Greg Romaniuk, Joel Larway, Travis Way, Doug Kauffman
2000	Wisconsin	Craig Brown (S), Ryan Quinn, Jon Brunt, JohnDunlop
1999	Wisconsin	Tim Somerville (S), Don Barcome Jr., Myles Brundidge, John Gordon, Bud Somerville
1998	Wisconsin	Paul Pustovar (S), Dave Violette, Greg Wilson, Cory Ward
1997	North Dakota	Craig Disher (S), Kevin Kakela, Joel Jacobson, Paul Peterson
1996	Wisconsin	Tim Somerville (S), Mike Schneeberger, Myles Brundidge, John Gordon
1995	Wisconsin	Tim Somerville (S), Mike Schneeberger, Myles Brundidge, John Gordon
1994	Minnesota	Scott Baird (S), Pete Fenson, Mark Haluptzok, Tim Johnson
1993	Minnesota	Scott Baird (S), Pete Fenson, Mark Haluptzok, Tim Johnson
1992	Washington	Doug Jones (S), Jason Larway, Joel Larway, Tom Violette

United States Curling Championships — Men's, continued

Year	Team	Members
1991	Wisconsin	Steve Brown (S), Paul Pustovar, George Godfrey, Wally Henry, Mike Fraboni
1990	Washington	Bard Nordlund (S), Doug Jones, Murphy Tomlinson, Tom Violette
1989	Washington	Jim Vukich (S), Curt Fish, Bard Nordlund, James Pleasants, Jason Larway
1988	Washington	Doug Jones (S), Bard Nordlund, Murphy Tomlinson, Mike Grennan
1987	Washington	Jim Vukich (S), Ron Sharpe, George Pepelnjak, Gary Joraanstad
1986	Wisconsin	Steve Brown (S), Wally Henry, George Godfrey, Richard Maskel
1985	Illinois	Tim Wright (S), John Jahant, Jim Wilson, Russ Armstrong
1984	Minnesota	Joe Roberts (S), Bruce Roberts, Gary Kleffman, Jerry Scott
1983	Colorado	Don Cooper (S), Jerry Van Brunt Jr., Bill Shipstad, Jack McNelly
1982	Wisconsin	Steve Brown (S), Ed Sheffield, Huns Gustrowsky, George Godfrey
1981	Wisconsin	Bob Nichols (S), Bud Somerville, Bob Christman, Robert Buchanan
1980	Minnesota	Paul Pustovar (S), John Jankilla, Gary Klefman, Jerry Scott
1979	Minnesota	Scott Baird (S), Dan Haluptzok, Mark Haluptzok, Bob Fenson
1978	Wisconsin	Bob Nichols (S), Bill Strum, Tom Locken, Bob Christman
1977	Minnesota	Bruce Roberts (S), Paul Pustovar, Gary Kleffman, Jerry Scott
1976	Minnesota	Bruce Roberts (S), Joe Roberts, Gary Kleffman, Jerry Scott
1975	Washington	Ed Risling (S), Charles Lundgren, Gary Schnee, Dave Tellvik

United States Curling Championships — Men's, continued

Year	Team	Members
1974	Wisconsin	Bud Somerville (S), Bob Nichols, Bill Strum, Tom Locken
1973	Massachusetts	Charles Reeves (S), Doug Carlson, Henry Shean, Barry Blanchard
1972	North Dakota	Bob Labonte (S), Frank Aasand, John Aasand, Ray Morgan
1971	North Dakota	Dale Dalziel (S), Dennis Melland, Clark Sampson, Rodney Melland
1970	North Dakota	Art Tallackson (S), Glenn Gilleshammer, Ray Holt, Trueman Thompson
1969	Wisconsin	Bud Somerville (S), Bill Strum, Franklin Bradshaw, Gene Ovesen
1968	Wisconsin	Bud Somerville (S), Bill Strum, Al Gagne, Tom Wright
1967	Washington	Bruce Roberts (S), Tom Fitzpatrick, John Wright, Doug Walker
1966	North Dakota	Bruce Roberts (S), Joe Zbacnik, Gerry Toutant, Mike O'Leary
1965	Wisconsin	Bud Somerville (S), Bill Strum, Al Gagne, Tom Wright
1964	Minnesota	Robert Magie Jr. (S), Bert Payne, Russell Barber, Britton Payne
1963	Michigan	Mike Slyziuk (S), Nelson Brown, Ernest Slyziuk, Walter Hubchik
1962	Minnesota	Dick Brown (S), Terry Kleffman, Fran Kleffman, Nick Jerulle
1961	Washington	Frank Crealock (S), Ken Sherwood, John Jamieson, Bud McCartney
1960	North Dakota	Orvil Gilleshammer (S), Glenn Gilleshammer, Wilmer Collette, Donald Labonte
1959	Minnesota	Dick Brown (S), Terry Kleffman, Fran Kleffman, Nick Jerulle
1958	Michigan	Mike Slyziuk (S), Douglas Fisk, Ernest Slyziuk, Merritt Knowlson
1957	Minnesota	Harold Lauber (S), Louis Lauber, Peter Beasy, Matt Berklich

United States Curling Championships — Women's

Year	Team	Members
2008	Wisconsin	Debbie McCormick (S), Allison Pottinger, Nicole Joraanstad, Natalie Nicholson
2007	Wisconsin	Debbie McCormick (S), Allison Pottinger, Nicole Joraanstad, Natalie Nicholson, Tracy Sachtjen
2006	Wisconsin	Debbie McCormick (S), Allison Pottinger, Nicole Joraanstad, Natalie Nicholson
2005	Minnesota	Cassie Johnson (S), Jamie (Johnson) Haskell, Jessica Schultz, Maureen Brunt
2004	Wisconsin	Patti Lank (S), Erika Brown, Nicole Joraanstad, Natalie Nicholson
2003	Wisconsin	Debbie McCormick (S), Allison Pottinger, Ann Swisshelm Silver, Tracy Sachtjen
2002	Wisconsin	Patti Lank (S), Erika Brown, Allison Pottinger, Natalie Nicholson, Nicole Joraanstad
2001	Illinois	Kari Erickson (S), Debbie McCormick, Stacey Liapis, Ann Swisshelm Silver
2000	Nebraska	Amy Wright (S), Amy Becher, Joni Cotten, Natalie Nicholson, Corina Marquardt
1999	Wisconsin	Patti Lank (S), Erika Brown, Allison Pottinger, Tracy Sachtjen
1998	Illinois	Kari Erickson (S), Lori Kreklau, Stacey Liapis, Ann Swisshelm Silver
1997	Wisconsin	Patti Lank (S), Analissa Johnson, Joni Cotten, Tracy Sachtjen
1996	Wisconsin	Lisa Schoeneberg (S), Erika Brown, Lori Mountford, Allison Pottinger, Debbie McCormick
1995	Wisconsin	Lisa Schoeneberg (S), Erika Brown, Lori Mountford, Marcia Tillisch, Allison Pottinger
1994	Colorado	Bev Behnke (S), Dawna Bennett, Susan Anschuetz, Pam Finch
1993	Colorado	Bev Behnke (S), Dawna Bennett, Susan Anschuetz, Pam Finch

United States Curling Championships — Women's, continued

Year	Team	Members
1992	Wisconsin	Lisa Schoeneberg (S), Amy Wright, Lori Mountford, Jill Jones
1991	Texas	Maymar Gemmell (S), Judy Johnston, Janet Hunter, Brenda Jancic
1990	Colorado	Bev Behnke (S), Dawna Bennett, Susan Anschuetz, Pam Finch
1989	North Dakota	Jan Legacie (S), Janie Kakela, Cooky Bertsch, Eileen Mickelson
1988	Washington	Nancy Richard (S), Nancy Pearson, Leslie Frosch, Mary Hobson
1987	Washington	Sharon Good (S), Joan Fish, Beth Bronger-Jones, Aija Edwards
1986	Minnesota	Gerri Tilden (S), Linda Barneson, Barb Polski, Barb Gutzmer
1985	Alaska	Bev Birklid (S), Peggy Martin, Jerry Evans, Katrina Sharp
1984	Minnesota	Amy Wright (S), Terry Leksell, Karen Leksell, Kelly Sieger
1983	Washington	Nancy Richard (S), Dolores Campbell, Nancy Pearson, Leslie Frosch
1982	Illinois	Ruth Schwenker (S), Stephanie Flynn, Donna Purkey, Kathleen Wilson
1981	Washington	Nancy Richard (S), Carol Dahl, Leslie Frosch, Nancy Wallace
1980	Washington	Sharon Kozai (S), Joan Fish, Betty Kozai, Aija Edwards
1979	Washington	Nancy Richard (S), Dolores Campbell, Leslie Frosch, Nancy Wallace
1978	Wisconsin	Sandy Robarge (S), Elaine Collins, Jo Shannon, Virginia Morrison
1977	New York	Margaret Smith (S), Cynthia Smith, Jackie Grant, Eve Switzer

World Curling Championships — Men's

2008

FINAL

Nation	1	2	3	4	5	6	7	8	9	10	Total
Canada	0	1	0	0	2	0	1	0	2	x	6
Scotland	0	0	1	0	0	0	0	2	0	x	3

P	Canada	%
L	Ben Hebert	85
2	Marc Kennedy	95
3	John Morris	95
S	Kevin Martin	89

P	Scotland	%
L	Euan Byers	95
2	Peter Smith	78
3	Graeme Connal	88
S	David Murdoch	78

BRONZE

Nation	1	2	3	4	5	6	7	8	9	10	Total
China	0	0	0	0	2	0	0	1	0	x	3
Norway	2	0	0	0	0	3	2	0	1	x	8

P	China	%
L	Jia Liang Zang	92
2	Xiao Ming Xu	85
3	Rui Liu	85
S	Fengchun Wang	68

P	Norway	%
L	Håvard Petersson	99
2	Christoffer Svae	80
3	Torger Nergård	84
S	Thomas Ulsrud	88

Round-robin Standings

Nation	W	L
Canada	10	1
Scotland	8	3
China	7	4
Norway	7	4
France	6	5
Australia	5	6

Nation	W	L
USA	5	6
Germany	5	6
Denmark	4	7
Sweden	4	7
Switzerland	3	8
Czech Republic	2	9

World Curling Championships — Men's, continued

2007

FINAL

Nation	1	2	3	4	5	6	7	8	9	10	Total
Canada	4	0	0	1	0	3	0	0	x	x	8
Germany	0	0	1	0	0	0	0	1	x	x	3

P	Canada	%
L	Craig Savill	92
2	Brent Laing	86
3	Richard Hart	98
S	Glenn Howard	98

P	Germany	%
L	Andreas Kempf	91
2	Andreas Lang	78
3	Ulrich Kapp	72
S	Andreas Kapp	80

BRONZE

Nation	1	2	3	4	5	6	7	8	9	10	Total
USA	0	0	1	0	1	0	2	0	0	0	4
Gormany	1	0	0	2	0	1	0	1	0	1	6

P	USA	%
L	Kevin Birr	80
2	Greg Johnson	91
3	Bill Todhunter	78
S	Todd Birr	73

P	Germany	%
L	Andreas Kempf	89
2	Andreas Lang	84
3	Ulrich Kapp	89
S	Andreas Kapp	85

Round-robin Standings

Nation	W	L
Canada	10	1
USA	8	3
Switzerland	7	4
Germany	6	5
Sweden	6	5
Finland	6	5

Nation	W	L
France	6	5
Norway	4	7
Scotland	4	7
Australia	4	7
Denmark	4	7
Korea	1	10

World Curling Championships — Men's, continued

2006

FINAL

Nation	1	2	3	4	5	6	7	8	9	10	Total
Canada	0	1	0	1	0	2	0	0	0	x	4
Scotland	1	0	1	0	2	0	0	2	1	x	7

P	Canada	%
L	Maxime Elmaleh	85
2	Éric Sylvain	76
3	François Roberge	72
S	Jean-Michel Ménard	76

P	Scotland	%
L	Euan Byers	81
2	Warwick Smith	82
3	Ewan MacDonald	86
S	David Murdoch	87

BRONZE

Nation	1	2	3	4	5	6	7	8	9	10	Total
Scotland	0	1	0	0	2	0	1	0	0	2	6
Norway	0	0	2	1	0	0	0	0	1	0	4

P	Scotland	%
L	Euan Byers	74
2	Warwick Smith	73
3	Ewan MacDonald	68
S	David Murdoch	75

P	Norway	%
L	Jan Thoreson	75
2	Thomas Due	68
3	Torger Nergård	69
S	Thomas Ulsrud	68

Round-robin Standings

Nation	W	L	Nation	W	L
Scotland	9	2	Switzerland	6	5
Canada	8	3	Denmark	5	6
Norway	7	4	Australia	5	6
USA	7	4	Germany	4	7
Finland	6	5	Japan	2	9
Sweden	6	5	Ireland	1	10

World Curling Championships — Men's, continued

2005

FINAL

Nation	1	2	3	4	5	6	7	8	9	10	Total
Scotland	0	2	0	0	1	0	0	1	x	x	4
Canada	1	0	5	0	0	0	5	0	x	x	11

P	Scotland	%
L	Euan Byers	86
2	Neil Murdoch	83
3	Craig Wilson	81
S	David Murdoch	67

P	Canada	%
L	Marcel Rocque	93
2	Scott Pfeifer	84
S	Randy Ferbey	89
4	David Nedohin	95

BRONZE

Nation	1	2	3	4	5	6	7	8	9	10	Total
Canada	2	0	0	0	2	0	1	0	0	3	8
Gormany	0	2	0	1	0	1	0	1	1	0	6

P	Canada	%
L	Marcel Rocque	88
2	Scott Pfeifer	81
S	Randy Ferbey	86
4	David Nedohin	79

P	Germany	%
L	Andreas Kempf	84
2	Oliver Axnick	76
3	Ulrich Kapp	76
S	Andreas Kapp	81

Round-robin Standings

Nation	W	L
Scotland	8	3
Germany	8	3
Norway	8	3
Canada	8	3
Finland	8	3
USA	8	3

Nation	W	L
Switzerland	6	5
New Zealand	5	6
Sweden	3	8
Australia	2	9
Denmark	1	10
Italy	1	10

World Curling Championship Winners — Men's

Year	Team	Members
2008	Canada	Kevin Martin (S), Ben Hebert, Marc Kennedy, John Morris, Adam Enright
2007	Canada	Glenn Howard (S), Richard Hart, Brent Laing, Craig Savill, Steve Bice
2006	Scotland	David Murdoch (S), Euan Byers, Warwick Smith, Ewan MacDonald, Peter Smith
2005	Canada	Randy Ferbey (S), David Nedohin, Marcel Rocque, Scott Pfeifer, Dan Holowaychuk
2004	Sweden	Peja Lindholm (S), Tomas Nordin, Magnus Swartling, Peter Narup, Anders Kraupp
2003	Canada	Randy Ferbey (S), David Nedohin, Scott Pfeifer, Marcel Rocque, Don Holowaychuk
2002	Canada	Randy Ferbey (S), David Nedohin, Scott Pfeifer, Marcel Rocque, Don Holowaychuk
2001	Sweden	Peja Lindholm (S), Tomas Nordin, Magnus Swartling, Peter Narup, Anders Kraupp
2000	Canada	Greg McAulay (S), Brent Pierce, Bryan Miki, Jody Sveistrup, Darin Fenton
1999	Scotland	Hammy McMillan (S), Warwick Smith, Ewan McDonald, Peter Loudon, Gordon Muirhead
1998	Canada	Wayne Middaugh (S), Graeme McCarrell, Ian Tetley, Scott Bailey, Dave Carruthers
1997	Sweden	Peja Lindholm (S), Tomas Nordin, Magnus Swartling, Peter Narup, Marcus Feldt
1996	Canada	Jeff Stoughton (S), Ken Tresoor, Garry Van Den Berghe, Steve Gould, Darryl Gunnlaugson
1995	Canada	Kerry Burtnyk (S), Jeff Ryan, Rob Meakin, Keith Fenton, Denis Fillion
1994	Canada	Rick Folk (S), Pat Ryan, Bert Gretzinger, Gerry Richard, Ron Steinhauer
1993	Canada	Russ Howard (S), Glenn Howard, Wayne Middaugh, Peter Corner, Larry Merkley
1992	Switzerland	Markus Eggler (S), Frédéric Jean, Stefan Hofer, Björn Schröder

World Curling Championship Winners — Men's, continued

Year	Team	Members
1991	Scotland	David Smith (S), Graeme Connal, Peter Smith, David Hay, Mike Hay
1990	Canada	Ed Werenich (S), John Kawaja, Ian Tetley, Pat Perroud, Neil Harrison
1989	Canada	Pat Ryan (S), Randy Ferbey, Don Walchuk, Don McKenzie, Murray Ursuliak
1988	Norway	Eigil Ramsfjell (S), Sjur Loen, Morten Søgaard, Bo Bakke
1987	Canada	Russ Howard (S), Glenn Howard, Tim Belcourt, Kent Carstairs
1986	Canada	Ed Lukowich (S), John Ferguson, Neil Houston, Brent Syme
1985	Canada	Al Hackner (S), Rick Lang, Ian Tetley, Pat Perroud
1984	Norway	Eigil Ramsfjell (S), Sjur Loen, Gunnar Meland, Bo Bakke
1983	Canada	Ed Werenich (S), Paul Savage, John Kawaja, Neil Harrison
1982	Canada	Al Hackner (S), Rick Lang, Bob Nicol, Bruce Kennedy
1981	Switzerland	Jürg Tanner (S), Jürg Hornisberger, Patrik Lörtscher, Franz Tanner
1980	Canada	Rick Folk (S), Ron Mills, Tom Wilson, Jim Wilson
1979	Norway	Kristian Sørum (S), Morten Sørum, Eigil Ramsfjell, Gunnar Meland
1978	United States	Bob Nichols (S), Bill Strum, Tom Locken, Bob Christman
1977	Sweden	Ragnar Kamp (S), Håkan Rudström, Björn Rudström, Christer Mårtensson
1976	United States	Bruce Roberts (S), Joe Roberts, Gery Kleffman, Jerry Scott
1975	Switzerland	Otto Danieli (S), Roland Schneider, Rolf Gautschi, Ueli Mülli

World Curling Championship Winners — Men's, continued

Year	Team	Members
1974	United States	Bud Somerville (S), Bob Nichols, Bill Strum, Tom Locken
1973	Sweden	Kjell Oscarius (S), Bengt Oscarius, Tom Schaeffer, Boa Carlman
1972	Canada	Orest Meleschuk (S), Dave Romaro, John Hanesiak, Pat Hailley
1971	Canada	Don Duguid (S), Rod Hunter, Jim Pettapiece, Bryan Wood
1970	Canada	Don Duguid (S), Rod Hunter, Jim Pettapiece, Bryan Wood
1969	Canada	Ron Northcott (S), Jimmy Shields, Bernie Sparkes, Fred Storey
1968	Canada	Ron Northcott (S), Jimmy Shields, Bernie Sparkes, Fred Storey
1967	Scotland	Chuck Hay (S), John Bryden, Alan Glen, David Howie
1966	Canada	Ron Northcott (S), George Fink, Bernie Sparkes, Fred Storey
1965	United States	Bud Somerville (S), Bill Strum, Al Gagne, Tom Wright
1964	Canada	Lyall Dagg (S), Leo Hebert, Fred Britton, Barry Naimark
1963	Canada	Ernie Richardson (S), Arnold Richardson, Sam Richardson, Mel Perry
1962	Canada	Ernie Richardson (S), Arnold Richardson, Sam Richardson, Wes Richardson
1961	Canada	Hec Gervais (S), Ray Werner, Vic Raymer, Wally Ursuliak
1960	Canada	Ernie Richardson (S), Arnold Richardson, Sam Richardson, Wes Richardson
1959	Canada	Ernie Richardson (S), Arnold Richardson, Sam Richardson, Wes Richardson

World Curling Championships — Women's

2008

FINAL

Nation	1	2	3	4	5	6	7	8	9	10	Total
Canada	0	3	0	1	0	0	2	0	1	x	7
China	1	0	1	0	1	0	0	1	0	x	4

P	Canada	%
L	Dawn Askin	90
2	Jill Officer	89
3	Cathy Overton-Clapham	86
S	Jennifer Jones	85

P	China	%
L	Yan Zhou	84
2	Qingshuang Yue	85
3	Yin Liu	70
S	Bingyu Wang	81

BRONZE

Nation	1	2	3	4	5	6	7	8	9	10	Total
Japan	0	2	0	0	0	2	1	2	0	x	7
Switzerland	3	0	2	2	1	0	0	0	1	x	9

P	Japan	%
L	Kotomi Ishizaki	91
2	Mayo Yamaura	88
3	Mari Motohashi	81
S	Moe Meguro	54

P	Switzerland	%
L	Janine Greiner	91
2	Valeria Spälty	79
3	Carmen Schäfer	86
S	Mirjam Ott	73

Round-robin Standings

Nation	W	L
China	9	2
Canada	9	2
Switzerland	9	2
Japan	7	4
Denmark	7	4
Sweden	6	5

Nation	W	L
USA	6	5
Russia	4	7
Germany	4	7
Scotland	3	8
Italy	2	9
Czech Republic	0	11

World Curling Championships — Women's, continued

2007

FINAL

Nation	1	2	3	4	5	6	7	8	9	10	Total
Denmark	0	1	0	2	0	0	0	1	0	x	4
Canada	2	0	1	0	1	1	2	0	1	x	8

P	Denmark	%
L	Ane Hansen	86
2	Angelina Jensen	77
3	Denise Dupont	72
S	Madeleine Dupont	71

P	Canada	%
L	Renee Simmons	81
2	Sasha Carter	82
3	Jeanna Schraeder	86
S	Kelly Scott	87

BRONZE

Nation	1	2	3	4	5	6	7	8	9	10	Total
Denmark	0	1	0	0	1	0	2	2	1	1	9
Scotland	1	0	3	1	0	1	0	0	0	0	6

P	Denmark	%
L	Ane Hansen	50
2	Angelina Jensen	58
3	Denise Dupont	69
S	Madeleine Dupont	72

P	Scotland	%
L	Lindsay Wood	83
2	Lorna Vevers	63
3	Jackie Lockhart	69
S	Kelly Wood	70

Round-robin Standings

Nation	W	L
Canada	10	1
Denmark	8	3
Scotland	8	3
USA	7	4
Switzerland	6	5
Sweden	6	5

Nation	W	L
China	5	6
Germany	4	7
Japan	4	7
Russia	4	7
Czech Republic	2	9
Italy	2	9

World Curling Championships — Women's, continued

2006

FINAL

Nation	1	2	3	4	5	6	7	8	9	10	Total
Sweden	1	0	2	0	3	1	0	2	0	1	10
USA	0	1	0	4	0	0	2	0	2	0	9

P	Sweden	%
L	Anna Svärd	86
2	Catherine Lindahl	76
3	Eva Lund	79
S	Anette Norberg	76

P	USA	%
L	Natalie Nicholson	88
2	Nicole Joraanstad	80
3	Allison Pottinger	83
S	Debbie McCormick	75

BRONZE

Nation	1	2	3	4	5	6	7	8	9	10	Total
Canada	0	2	1	0	0	1	0	2	1	0	7
USA	3	0	0	2	0	0	1	0	0	2	8

P	Canada	%
L	Renee Simmons	81
2	Sasha Carter	74
3	Jeanna Schraeder	84
S	Kelly Scott	75

P	USA	%
L	Natalie Nicholson	84
2	Nicole Joraanstad	78
3	Allison Pottinger	75
S	Debbie McCormick	73

Round-robin Standings

Nation	W	L
Sweden	10	1
USA	10	1
Germany	8	3
Canada	7	4
China	6	5
Denmark	6	5

Nation	W	L
Norway	5	6
Scotland	4	7
Italy	4	7
Switzerland	3	8
Japan	3	8
Netherlands	0	11

World Curling Championships — Women's, continued

2005

FINAL

Nation	1	2	3	4	5	6	7	8	9	10	Total
Sweden	0	0	0	1	0	0	3	0	2	4	10
USA	0	0	1	0	1	1	0	1	0	0	4

P	Sweden	%
L	Anna Bergstöm	89
2	Catherine Lindahl	70
3	Eva Lund	83
S	Anette Norberg	78

P	USA	%
L	Maureen Brunt	88
2	Jessica Schultz	78
3	Jamie Johnson	73
S	Cassandra Johnson	64

BRONZE

Nation	1	2	3	4	5	6	7	8	9	10	Total
Sweden	3	1	0	1	0	3	2	0	x	x	10
Norway	0	0	1	0	2	0	0	1	x	x	4

P	Sweden	%
L	Anna Bergstöm	63
2	Catherine Lindahl	75
3	Eva Lund	92
S	Anette Norberg	60

P	Norway	%
L	Camilla Holth	53
2	Marianne Haslum	52
3	Linn Githmark	50
S	Dordi Nordby	55

Round-robin Standings

Nation	W	L	Nation	W	L
Sweden	11	0	China	4	7
USA	10	1	Switzerland	4	7
Canada	8	3	Japan	3	8
Norway	7	4	Denmark	3	8
Russia	7	4	Italy	2	9
Scotland	6	5	Finland	1	10

World Curling Championships Winners — Women's

Year	Team	Members
2008	Canada	Jennifer Jones (S), Dawn Askin, Jill Officer, Cathy Overton-Clapham, Jennifer Clarke-Rouire
2007	Canada	Kelly Scott (S), Renee Simons, Sasha Carter, Jeanna Schaeder, Michelle Allen
2006	Sweden	Anette Norberg (S), Anna Svard, Catherine Lindahl, Eva Lund, Ulrika Bergman
2005	Sweden	Anette Norberg (S), Anna Bergstrom, Catherine Lindahl, Eva Lund, Ulrika Bergman
2004	Canada	Colleen Jones (S), Kim Kelly, Mary-Anne Arsenault, Nancy Delahunt, Mary Sue Radford
2003	United States	Debbie McCormick (S), Allison Pottinger, Ann Swisshelm Silver, Tracy Sachtjen, Joni Cotten
2002	Scotland	Jackie Lockhart (S), Sheila Swan, Katriona Fairweather, Anne Laird, Edith Loudon
2001	Canada	Colleen Jones (S), Kim Kelly, Mary-Anne Waye, Nancy Delahunt, Laine Peters
2000	Canada	Kelley Law (S), Julie Skinner, Georgina Wheatcroft, Diane Nelson, Cheryl Noble
1999	Sweden	Elisabet Gustafson (S), Katarina Nyberg, Louise Marmont, Elisabeth Persson, Margaretha Lindahl
1998	Sweden	Elisabet Gustafson (S), Katarina Nyberg, Louise Marmont, Elisabeth Persson, Margaretha Lindahl
1997	Canada	Sandra Schmirler (S), Jan Betker, Joan McCusker, Marcia Gudereit, Atina Ford
1996	Canada	Marilyn Bodogh (S), Corie Beveridge, Kim Gellard, Jane Hooper-Perroud, Lisa Savage
1995	Sweden	Elisabet Gustafson (S), Katarina Nyberg, Louise Marmont, Elisabeth Persson, Helena Svensson
1994	Canada	Sandra Peterson (S), Jan Betker, Joan McCusker, Marcia Gudereit, Atina Ford

World Curling Championships Winners — Women's, continued

Year	Team	Members
1993	Canada	Sandra Peterson (S), Jan Betker, Joan McCusker, Marcia Gudereit, Atina Ford
1992	Sweden	Elisabet Johanssen (S), Katarina Nyberg, Louise Marmont, Elisabeth Persson, Annika Lööf
1991	Norway	Dordi Nordby (S), Hanne Pettersen, Mette Halvorsen, Anne Jøtun, Marianne Aspelin
1990	Norway	Dordi Nordby (S), Hanne Pettersen, Mette Halvorsen, Anne Bakke
1989	Canada	Heather Houston (S), Lorraine Lang, Diane Adams, Tracy Kennedy, Gloria Taylor
1988	Germany	Andrea Schöpp (S), Almut Scholl, Monika Wagner, Suzanne Fink
1987	Canada	Pat Sanders (S), Georgina Hawkes, Louise Herlinveau, Deb Massullo
1986	Canada	Marilyn Darte (S), Kathy McEdwards, Chris Jurgenson, Jan Augustyn
1985	Canada	Linda Moore (S), Lindsay Sparkes, Debbie Jones, Laurie Carney
1984	Canada	Connie Laliberte (S), Chris More, Corrine Peters, Janet Arnott
1983	Switzerland	Erika Müller (S), Barbara Meyer, Barbara Meier, Christina Wirz
1982	Denmark	Helena Blach (S), Mariane Jørgensen, Astrid Birmbaum, Jette Olsen
1981	Sweden	Elisabeth Högström (S), Carina Olsson, Birgitta Sewik, Karin Sjögren
1980	Canada	Marj Mitchell (S), Nancy Kerr, Shirley McKendry, Wendy Leach
1979	Switzerland	Gaby Casanova (S), Rosie Manger, Linda Thommen, Betty Bourgiun

World Curling Tour 2008 — Men's Standings

Rank	Name	Country	Points
1	Kevin Martin	Canada	623.050
2	Glenn Howard	Canada	589.700
3	Kevin Koe	Canada	449.350
4	Randy Ferbey	Canada	389.152
5	Kerry Burtnyk	Canada	347.472
6	Jeff Stoughton	Canada	333.300
7	Pat Simmons	Canada	329.250
8	Brad Gushue	Canada	302.086
9	Wayne Middaugh	Canada	240.065
10	David Murdoch	Scotland	183.800
11	Joel Jordison	Canada	174.225
12	Thomas Ulsrud	Norway	173.768
13	Peter Corner	Canada	155.919
14	Shawn Adams	Canada	139.450
15	Bob Ursel	Canada	133.107

World Curling Tour 2008 — Men's Money List

Rank	Name	Country	Money
1	Kevin Martin	Canada	$127,000
2	Glenn Howard	Canada	$126,795
3	Kevin Koe	Canada	$109,785
4	Wayne Middaugh	Canada	$83,500
5	Randy Ferbey	Canada	$76,750
6	Kerry Burtnyk	Canada	$73,729
7	Jeff Stoughton	Canada	$71,000
8	Pat Simmons	Canada	$55,000
9	Shawn Adams	Canada	$43,000
10	Bob Ursel	Canada	$42,500
	Greg McAulay	Canada	$42,500
12	Brad Gushue	Canada	$39,336
13	Joel Jordison	Canada	$26,000
14	Peter Corner	Canada	$24,900
15	Martin Ferland	Canada	$24,100

World Curling Tour 2008 — Women's Standings

Rank	Name	Country	Points
1	Jennifer Jones	Canada	450.050
2	Shannon Kleibrink	Canada	354.985
3	Kelly Scott	Canada	333.750
4	Cheryl Bernard	Canada	277.717
5	Stefanie Lawton	Canada	249.715
6	Sherry Anderson	Canada	232.383
7	Sherry Middaugh	Canada	212.625
8	Cathy King	Canada	202.899
9	Mirjam Ott	Switzerland	156.870
10	Anette Norberg	Sweden	151.599
11	Ludmilla Privivkova	Russia	129.088
12	Kelly Wood	Scotland	122.265
13	Krista McCarville (Scharf)	Canada	119.007
14	Michelle Englot	Canada	116.625
15	Amber Holland	Canada	96.083

World Curling Tour 2008 — Women's Money List

Rank	Name	Country	Money
1	Shannon Kleibrink	Canada	$53,179
2	Jennifer Jones	Canada	$47,205
3	Sherry Middaugh	Canada	$38,600
4	Stefanie Lawton	Canada	$37,000
5	Kelly Scott	Canada	$36,845
6	Cheryl Bernard	Canada	$33,400
7	Amber Holland	Canada	$31,300
8	Krista McCarville	Canada	$29,500
9	Eve Bélisle	Canada	$27,300
10	Sherry Anderson	Canada	$23,762
11	Michelle Englot	Canada	$23,500
12	Cathy King	Canada	$22,350
13	Mirjam Ott	Switzerland	$18,018
14	Kristie Moore	Canada	$15,450
15	Heather Rankin	Canada	$13,550

World Curling Rankings* — Men's

+-	Country	Rank	2008	Rank	2007
0	Canada	1	1038	1	1200
0	Scotland/GBR	2	724	2	782
1	Norway	3	639	4	758
-1	USA	4	636	3	779
2	Germany	5	542	7	656
-1	Finland	6	524	5	721
-1	Switzerland	7	497	6	680
0	Sweden	8	462	8	602
3	France	9	265	12	228
3	Australia	10	260	13	207
-2	Denmark	11	255	9	295
-2	Italy	12	251	10	294
-2	New Zealand	13	223	11	265
7	China	14	213	21	84
4	Czech Republic	15	123	19	106
4	Ireland	16	112	20	100
-2	Russia	17	112	15	117
-4	Japan	18	100	14	129
-3	Wales	19	104	16	117
-2	England	20	102	18	107
-4	Korea	21	95	17	109
2	Hungary	22	80	24	71
-1	Netherlands	23	79	22	83
1	Latvia	24	77	25	60
2	Spain	25	72	27	53
-3	Austria	26	62	23	77
-1	Bulgaria	27	50	26	59
5	Slovakia	28	49	33	36
-1	Belgium	29	48	28	49
-1	Chinese Taipei	30	40	29	44

World Curling Rankings — Men's, continued

+-	Country	Rank	2008	Rank	2007
0	Poland	31	39	31	39
0	Estonia	32	34	32	36
-3	Belarus	33	33	30	39
0	Greece	34	28	34	27
2	Croatia	35	27	37	14
0	Andorra	36	20	36	23
3	Lithuania	37	20	40	4,5
-3	Luxembourg	38	14	35	25
0	Serbia	39	11	39	8,5
-2	Kazakhstan	40	10	38	13
-	Iceland	41	4	-	-

World Curling Rankings* — Women's

+-	Country	Rank	2008	Rank	2007
0	Canada	1	928	1	1020
0	Sweden	2	795	2	1012
1	Switzerland	3	672	4	762
-1	USA	4	615	3	776
2	Denmark	5	521	7	583
-1	Scotland/GBR	6	506	5	724
-1	Norway	7	464	6	669
1	Japan	8	446	9	439
3	China	9	400	12	267
-2	Russia	10	398	8	465
-1	Italy	11	296	10	325
-1	Germany	12	275	11	323
0	Czech Republic	13	154	13	147
0	Finland	14	137	14	144

World Curling Rankings — Women's, continued

+-	Country	Rank	2008	Rank	2007
1	Netherlands	15	122	16	125
-1	Korea	16	121	15	127
0	England	17	109	17	104
2	Austria	18	106	20	88
-1	France	19	101	18	101
-1	New Zealand	20	87	19	95
1	Hungary	21	87	22	80
-1	Latvia	22	81	21	84
1	Poland	23	68	24	54
-1	Spain	24	65	23	71
2	Australia	25	54	27	42
3	Estonia	26	51	29	36
3	Croatia	27	48	30	32
0	Ireland	28	41	28	36
-4	Chinese Taipei	29	38	25	53
1	Slovakia	30	38	31	29
4	Lithuania	31	31	35	15
-6	Bulgaria	32	27	26	44
-1	Andorra	33	19	32	27
-1	Kazakhstan	34	16	33	23
-1	Wales	35	16	34	22

*Created by the World Curling Association in 2006, these standings are used to rank the success of member associations. Point values are assigned to top-level placements at competitions, including the Olympics and World Curling Championships. Point values diminish for events in the previous five curling seasons. The rankings are updated each March.

Notes on Sources

Book Sources

Clark, Doug. *The Roaring Game: A Sweeping Saga of Curling.* Toronto: Key Porter Books Limited, 2007.

Hansen, Warren. *Curling: The History, The Players, The Game.* Toronto: Key Porter Books, 1999.

Jones, Terry. *The Ferbey Four.* Edmonton: Dragon Hill Publishing, 2007.

Lukowich, Ed, with Rick Folk and Paul Gowsell. *The Curling Book: With Tips for Beginners and Experts.* Douglas & McIntyre, 2004.

Maxwell, Doug. *Tales of a Curling Hack.* North Vancouver: Whitecap Books Ltd., 2006.

Maxwell, Doug. *Canada Curls: The Illustrated History of Curling in Canada.* North Vancouver: Whitecap Books Ltd., 2002.

Maxwell, Doug, ed. *The First Fifty: A Nostalgic Look at the Brier.* Toronto: Maxcurl Publications, 1980.

Russell, Scott. *Open House: Canada and the Magic of Curling.* Toronto: Doubleday, 2003.

Weeks, Bob. *Curling for Dummies.* 2nd ed. Toronto: For Dummies, 2006.

Web Sources

http://archives.cbc.ca/sports/curling/topics/550-2821/

http://communities.canada.com/calgaryherald/blogs/curling/archive/2008/06/25/great-news-for-the-cca.aspx

http://curlnews.blogspot.com/2006/09/asham-world-curling-tour-announced.html

http://curlnews.blogspot.com/2006/09/cbc-slams-back-into-curling.html

http://curlnews.blogspot.com/2008/06/curling-ice-king-hospitalized.html

http://deangemmell.com/bio.php

http://en.wikipedia.org

http://en.wikipedia.org/wiki/Colleen_Jones

http://en.wikipedia.org/wiki/Guy_Hemmings

http://en.wikipedia.org/wiki/Jack_Wells

http://en.wikipedia.org/wiki/Randy_Ferbey

http://en.wikipedia.org/wiki/Russ_Howard

http://en.wikipedia.org/wiki/Sandra_Schmirler

http://en.wikipedia.org/wiki/The_Battle_of_the_Sexes_(Tennis)

http://en.wikipedia.org/wiki/The_Black_Bonspiel_of_Wullie_MacCrimmon

http://en.wikipedia.org/wiki/World_Curling_Tour

http://icing.org/game/history/historya.htm

http://library.thinkquest.org/26974/e_history.htm

http://rockstarcurling.com/

http://seasonofchampions.ca/2008continentalcup/news114.asp

http://slam.canoe.ca/Slam/Columnists/Jones/2005/11/01/1287835-sun.html

http://slam.canoe.ca/Slam/Curling/2005/11/01/1287837-sun.html

http://slam.canoe.ca/Slam/Curling/2007/01/08/pf-3235758.html

http://slam.canoe.ca/Slam/Curling/Brier/2007/03/11/3731256-sun.html

http://theatreinlondon.ca/old/site/reviews/2004_reviews/Black_Bonspiel.htm

http://www.canada.com/vancouversun/features/2010/story.html?id=d09a9132-7cf0-489f-900f-9d9f42722b89

http://www.cbc.ca/sports/curling/story/2008/01/16/wct-boutilier.html

http://www.cbc.ca/sports/curling/story/2008/04/13/martin-worldcurling-final.html

http://www.cbc.ca/sports/indepth/feature-colleen-jones-qa.html

http://www.collectionscanada.gc.ca/curling/index-e.html

http://www.cshof.ca/hm_profile.php?i=188

http://www.curlingrichardsons.com/index.htm

http://www.curlingrussia.com/eng/index-6.html

http://www.englishcurlingforum.com/viewtopic.php?t=452&s id=1aed773f340754a5db2be92e791b9ec9

http://www.gutenberg.org/ebooks/18619

http://www.halifax.ca/history/titanic.html

http://www.inthehack.com/forum/ice_makers/shorty_jenkins

http://www.mayflowercc.com/

http://www.nationalpost.com/sports/story.html?id=399094

http://www.nationalpost.com/sports/story.html?id=401676

http://www.nodice.ca/curling/

http://www.quotegarden.com/olympics-winter.html

http://www.richardsonlighting.com/html/about.html

http://www.robertburns.org/works/141.shtml

http://www.royalcaledoniancurlingclub.org

http://www.sportsnet.ca/more/2008/02/14/scotties_kelly_ scott/

http://www.teamkevinmartin.com/team/team.htm

http://www.thecurlingshow.com/

http://www.thecurlingshow.com/curlingshows/Ferbey2_Curl- ingShow.mp3

http://www.theglobeandmail.com/servlet/story/ LAC.20080204.WEEKS04/TPStory/TPSports/?query=

http://www.thestreaker.org.uk/main.htm

http://www.usacurl.org/usacurl//index.php?option=com_cont ent&task=view&id=12&Itemid=29

http://www.winnipegfreepress.com/sports/brier/story/ 4143969p-4734318c.html

http://www.worldcurling.org/content/blogsection/5/81/

http://www.worldcurlingtour.com/

http://www1.curling.ca/

http://www3.sympatico.ca/goweezer/canada/titanic.htm

Carla MacKay

Raised in Espanola, Ontario, Carla has always been a book lover, keeping track of every book she has read since she was 10 years old. So, when the opportunity to contribute to a book came around, she enthusiastically jumped in. She loved sports growing up, including curling, and drew on memories of her bonspiels to get her through the nuances of curling stats and the differences between an iron curling stone and a granite one. Carla is an avid runner and has completed two marathons. She lives in Edmonton with her longtime beau.

Geoffrey Lansdell

Geoffrey Lansdell is a pulp culture writer who grew up in Victoria, BC. For the past 10 years he has lived in Montréal, Québec, where he has worked at a variety of jobs from nightclub cigar salesman to mosaicist and telemarketer for a sinister company. He earned two BA degrees from Concordia University, one in Creative Writing, and one in the History of Western Society and Culture. Geoffrey now works as a freelance writer and ESL teacher. In life, he follows the advice of legendary curling journalist Cactus Jack Wells, who once said that it is "foolish to let the facts spoil a good story." With that in mind, he has written *Weird Facts About Curling*.